AN ILLUSTRATED GUIDE TO
MODERN
ELITE
FORCES

a Salamander book

Published by Arco Publishing, Inc.
NEW YORK

AN ILLUSTRATED GUIDE TO
MODERN
ELITE
FORCES

Max Walmer

A Salamander Book

Published by
Arco Publishing Inc.,
215 Park Avenue South,
New York, NY 10003,
United States of America.

© 1984 by Salamander Books Ltd.,
Salamander House,
27 Old Gloucester Street,
London WC1N 3AF,
United Kingdom.

ISBN 0 668 06064 6

Credits

Author: Max Walmer is a defense journalist who has contributed numerous articles to international defense journals.

Editor: Ray Bonds.

Designer: Philip Gorton.

Figure artworks: Rick Scollins.
Maps and diagrams: Alan Hollingbery and TIGA.

Picture research: Tony Moore.
Filmset by Modern Text Typesetting Ltd.
Color reproduction by Rodney Howe Ltd.
Printed in Belgium by Henri Proost et Cie.

Photographs: The publisher wishes to thank all the official government archives and individuals who have supplied pictures for this book. Photograph agencies only are credited on the page their pictures appear.

The forces included in this book have been selected as examples of particular elitism because their size, role or organisation makes them of special interest. Inevitably, there are elite forces which have been omitted and which some readers would have included, but space has prevented coverage of such a vast subject in a totally comprehensive way.

Also, in selected cases, there are descriptions which show how some of the forces have had to deal with very special problems, or carried out routine military operations in an exemplary manner.

Contents

Special Air Services

The Australian SAS Regiment was formed in July 1957 as 1st SAS Company. It was the first ever Australian special forces unit, and was clearly based upon the lessons learned in the Malayan campaign, which was then winding down. In 1960 the unit was transferred into the Royal Australian Regiment, the regular infantry element of the Australian Army. On September 4, 1964, the unit became independent again, was increased in size, and became the Australian Special Air Service Regiment.

1 SAS Squadron of the regiment deployed to Brunei in 1965 as part of the force countering Indonesian "confrontation", followed later by 2 SAS Squadron which went to Borneo. At virtually the same time Australia became involved in the Vietnam War and the three SAS squadrons rotated through that country from 1966 to 1971. They established a considerable reputation for themselves in Vietnam, serving mostly in Phuoc Tuy province to the south-east of the capital, Saigon.

The Australian SAS has not deployed operationally since the end of the Vietnam War (at least as far as public knowledge is concerned). But it is of considerable interest that, despite the very small size of the current Australian Army —they have only six regular battalions, for example— they still retain the SAS Regiment.

Organisation

At the height of the Vietnam and Confrontation campaigns the Australian SAS Regiment comprised: a headquarters; a Base Squadron; 1, 2 and 3 SAS Squadrons; and elements of 151 Signal Squadron. Since the war there has been slight reduction with the disbandment of 2 SAS Squadron; the rest remain.

Selection and training

Like the British SAS, the Australian SAS selects men from volunteers from other Army units; there is no recruiting direct from civilian life. Selection methods, too, are similar, but as there is no Australian marine corps there is a stronger emphasis on maritime activities.

Uniform

The Australian SAS Regiment personnel wear standard Australian Army uniform. Rather than the famous slouch-hat, however, they wear the equally famous sand-coloured beret and metal winged dagger badge of Britain's SAS. The wings, worn on the right sleeve, are also of the British SAS pattern.

1st Ranger Squadron, New Zealand SAS

The New Zealand Special Air Service Squadron was formed in 1954 to join the British and Rhodesian SAS in Malaya. As in Rhodesia, the initial volunteers were taken straight from civilian life and 138 were

Camouflage combat uniform

Sweatrag worn as combat hat

Bergen rucksack

Strap for canvas satchel

5.56mm M16A1 rifle

Pouch

Combat knife

M68 fragmentation grenade

Above: Australian SAS trooper on a jungle operation. He is armed with an M16A1 rifle and carries a "commando" knife.

accepted from a list of some 800. With 40 regular officers and NCOs, these were trained in New Zealand from June until November 1955 when the survivors were sent to Singapore to complete their parachute and jungle training. They soon deployed onto operations and spent 17 months out of the next two years in the jungle, killing 26 terrorists for the loss of just one of their own soldiers.

The squadron returned to New Zealand in November 1957 to be disbanded, but was resuscitated in August 1958. A troop of 30 men

Left: The New Zealand SAS has had jungle experience in Malaya, Borneo, Vietnam and Thailand, and still trains in Malaya.

was sent to Korat in Thailand from May to September 1962 in support of SEATO. In 1963 the unit was redesignated 1st Ranger Squadron, New Zealand Special Air Service, and shortly afterwards the unit deployed to Borneo where it served, once again, alongside the British SAS. It also operated from time to time with the Britain's SBS. 4 Troop NZSAS served in Vietnam from November 1968 to February 1971, where it served with the Australian SAS Squadron.

The unit is now stationed near Auckland in New Zealand. It has five troops and an HQ, with a separate small training establishment. Its task is to support New Zealand defence forces in their operations and, like the SAS in the United Kingdom, it has a major commitment to counter-terrorist missions. The uniform is standard New Zealand army, but badges are similar to those of the British SAS.

Special Service Force

Canada's Special Service Force is declared to NATO and is committed to the defence of North Norway as part of the Canadian Combined Air/Sea Transportable Brigade (CAST). In Norway the CAST would operate in conjunction with other allied formations such as the British/Netherlands Amphibious Force, the USMC Marines Amphibious Force and the Norweigan Army. Within Canada the Special Service Force concentrates on operations in the far north, and produces special rescue teams to deal with civilian emergencies.

The core of the Special Service Force is the Canadian Airborne Regiment, which is the elite unit of the Canadian armed forces. The airborne regiment can trace its origins back to the 1st Canadian Parachute Battalion, which was raised at Camp Shiloh in 1942, and the 2nd Parachute Battalion which later became part of the combined US/Canadian 1st Special Service Force (from which the modern force takes its name, even though there is no US involvement). The Canadian parachute force was maintained at a low level following World War II up to 1968 when the Canadian Airborne Regiment was formed to be a light, independent infantry unit for deployment in low-intensity operations.

Organisation

The Special Service Force is organised as a light brigade, although with only two infantry units its tactical viability is open to some question. Teeth arm units are an armoured regiment (8th Canadian Hussars), an infantry battalion (1st Battalion Royal Canadian Regiment) and the Canadian Airborne Regiment. Combat support comes from an airborne artillery regiment (2nd Royal Canadian Horse Artillery), an ▶

Right: The "Skyhawks" freefall parachute team is formed from men of the Canadian Airborne Regiment. Here they move towards joining up with the team leader.

Above: Trainees for the Airborne Regiment are checked out by the jumpmaster. No. 1 Airborne Commando consists entirely of French-Canadians.

Below: Gunners of 2nd Royal Canadian Horse Artillery bring their C-5 105mm pack-how into action. This is a local version of the Oto Melara Model 56.

engineer regiment and a signal squadron. Combat service support comes from the Airborne Service Commando (ie, logistic regiment).

The Canadian Airborne Regiment itself consists of three airborne commandos, which are equivalent to a company in size and organisation. 1st Airborne Commando is francophone (composed of French-Canadians), 2nd Airborne Commando is anglophone (English-Canadians), and 3rd is mixed.

Weapons and equipment

Small arms used by the Canadian Airborne Regiment include the US M16A1. However, there are also two Canadian adaptations of British weapons. First is the 9mm C1 sub-machine gun which is based on the Sterling L2A1, but has a simpler magazine (holding 30 as opposed to 34 rounds) and utilises the FN FAL bayonet. The most common rifle is the C1A1 7.62mm, which is modified from the L1A1 SLR to take a magazine charger and has a rotating disc rear sight.

The Squad Automatic Weapon is the heavy-barrelled version of the FN FAL, designated the C2A1 in Canadian service. The C2A1 can be recognised by the absence of a cover over the gas cylinder and barrel and the fitting of a bipod.

Uniform

The parade uniform is the bottle-green service dress with gold stripes for officers which is common to sea, land and air elements of the Canadian Armed Forces. Combat uniform is generally of US pattern (eg, helmets) but the NCOs' badges of rank are British. One unusual feature with the airborne troops is that the parachute qualification badge is a pair of wings surmounted by a maple leaf; for those serving with the Canadian Airborne Regiment the maple leaf is white, but for all others it is red. All eligible troops wear the paratroopers' red beret.

All members of the Special Service Force wear a patch with a winged sword and the motto "Osons" ("We Dare") clearly derived from that worn by the British SAS.

Below: Infantry soldier of the Special Service Force in winter gear. His rifle is the 7.62mm C1A1 version of the British SLR and is fitted for firing blanks.

Foreign Legion

No elite unit is surrounded by a more romantic image than the French Foreign Legion, and none is the subject of more misinformation and myth. Formed to help conquer and control Algeria (and also to clear riff-raff from the streets of Paris) the Legion's early days were troubled not only by repeated wars against Arabs, but also by ill-discipline and internal strife.

In 1835 the Legion was ceded in its entirety to Spain to "honour" a promise of aid, in a shabby and cynical political manoeuvre; of 5,000 despatched only 500 survived. Meanwhile a new Legion was formed in December 1835; it fought in North Africa, the Crimea (1854-56), Italy (1859), Mexico (1863-67), the Franco-Prussian war (1870) and in numerous colonial campaigns.

The Legion played a major role in both world wars, losing many men, but adding to its reputation. During World War I it lost 115 officers and 5,172 legionnaires killed in action and the Regiment de Marche de la Legion Etrangere became the most decorated unit in the French Army. The Legion even had units fighting each other in World War II, especially in Syria. After the war, the Legion fought in Indo-China, operating with great distinction in an increasingly disastrous campaign against the Viet Minh. During this period the first Legion parachute units were formed: *Bataillon Etranger de Parachutistes (BEP)*. The war culminated in the epic battle of Dien Bien Phu, one of the West's great military tragedies, where the 14,000 men of the French garrison (including no fewer than seven Legion battalions) were eventually totally overwhelmed (they never surrendered) on May 8, 1954.

No sooner was it out of Indo-China than the Legion found itself in another war, this time in Algeria. Six infantry regiments, two cavalry and two parachute regiments fought in Algeria, with four *Saharienne* companies, as always, operating in their deep penetration role.

Some Legion units took a few months off for the Anglo-French Suez campaign, but basically the Legion was involved in Algeria right up to the bitter end. Sadly, *1er Regiment Etranger de Parachutistes (1REP)* became involved in the generals' coup in 1961 and was disbanded in disgrace as a result.

The departure from Algeria has not, however, proved to be the end for the Legion, as had once been forecast, and since 1963 it has been heavily involved in many African countries, including Chad, Somaliland, Zaire, Djibouti and Malagasy. Units of the Legion also serve in the Pacific and in Central America.

Organisation

The French Foreign Legion exists today as an all-arms force, well equipped (with standard French Army weapons) and well organised to serve France. Its current organisation is based on regiments of 10 companies, with the specialist companies (reconnaissance, mortar, light armour, etc) increasing at the expense of the infantry companies —a trend by no means confined to the Legion, nor indeed to the French Army. Current major units are:

1er Regiment Etranger. Located at Caserne Vienot in Aubagne, this regiment is responsible for the administration of the whole Legion. It also runs the band, a company administering a large training camp, and in wartime produces three companies to defend the IRBM missile sites on the Plateau d'Albion.

2er Regiment Etranger d'Infantrie. a 1,500 strong infantry regiment based at Bonifacio, Corsica, its companies rotate through commando and other specialist schools and frequently serve on overseas detachments. ▶

Right: Paratrooper of the French Foreign Legion, one of the most famous of all elite units, which has fought in France's wars for 154 years with much distinction.

Green beret

Foreign Legion
parachute capbadge

French leather
webbing equipment

Pouch

Model 0F37
hand-grenade

Combat knife

9mm MAT 49
sub-machine gun.
Hand-grip also acts
as safety and although
his finger is on the
trigger the gun is
'safe'.

Canvas boots

13

▶ *3e Regiment Etranger d'Infantrie.* This regiment left Malagasy in 1973 and moved to its present base in Kourou, French Guiana.

4e Regiment Etranger. This regiment trains recruits and junior NCOs; it is located at Castelnaudary in France.

1er Regiment Etranger d'Cavalerie. Stationed at Orange, this regiment is the armoured component of the French Army's 14th Infantry Division. It consists of three armoured car squadrons and a lorried infantry company. It is also earmarked as one of the spearhead units of the French intervention force.

2e Regiment Etranger de Parachutistes. Stationed at Corte in Corsica, this regiment comprises and HQ and four combat companies. It prides itself in its ability to mount an operation against any given point in the world within 24 hours. One company is usually detached to *13DBLE.*

5e Regiment Mixte du Pacifique. Centred on Mururoa, the *RMP* has detachments at Tahiti and Arue. Its task is to provide security, communications and a power station for the French nuclear test sites in the Pacific. (As it includes French Army elements the regiment is designated *Mixte* rather than *Etranger.*)

61e Battaillon Mixte du Genie de la Legion. This engineer battalion was formed to prepare training areas, and is currently working on an arid site known as Les Causses

Rescue at Kolwezi May 1978

Following the widespread disorders after the granting of independence in 1960 and the resulting United Nations intervention, General Mobutu became President of Zaire in 1965. He had to deal with a succession of outbreaks of trouble in the following years, especially in Shaba province, formerly Katanga, the breakaway province once under the leadership of Möise Tshombe.

On May 13, 1978, a force of some 4,000 ''Tigers'' of the *Front National de Liberation du Congo* (FNLC) swept into Kolwezi, cutting its lines of communication with the capital, and inflicting heavy casualties on the Zairian army. There then followed an orgy of bloodshed and rape, and hundreds of Eruopean

Frank Spooner Pictures

in the Dordogne. The battalion comprises one Legion infantry company and one company of French Army engineers.

Detachment Legion Etrangere de Mayotte. This detachment of two companies, commanded by a lieutenant-colonel, is on the island of Mayotte in the Indian ocean. The island is a staging post on the route to Reunion and the 250-strong Legion unit guarantees its security.

Uniform

The Legion wears standard French Army uniforms, but with some special items to denote its status. The most famous item is the white-topped *kepi (kepi blanc)*, which is actually a white cloth cover on a standard blue *kepi* (with red top and gold badge and chin-strap). The *kepi blanc* cover is not worn by *sous* officers and above. Parade dress is khaki battledress with a number of ceremonial additions including green shoulder-boards with red tassels, white belt and gaiters, blue waist sash, and white gauntlets. A green tie is worn and officers also wear a green waistcoat. Members of the pioneer platoon wear a white apron and carry a ceremonial axe; they are also permitted to grow a beard.

Combat dress is the standard French camouflage suit, usually with a beret. Regiments on operations use a *foulard*, a strip of coloured cloth, to indicate companies. Foreign Legion parachutists wear the green beret.

---

men, women and children were murdered or kidnapped. On May 14 President Mobutu formally requested help from France, and to the credit of the French they responded both rapidly and effectively.

The rescue operation

On May 17, 1978, at about 1000 hours, 2nd Foreign Legion Parachute Regiment (2^{e}REP) at its base at Calvi in Corsica was placed at 6 hours notice to move. Executive orders did not arrive until 0130 hours the next morning and by 0800 hours the regiment was at the Solenzara airbase ready to go. The first echelon left that afternoon on five chartered DC-8 aircraft belonging to French civil airlines, to be followed later by the balance of the unit, together with the heavy weapons and vehicles, in USAF C-141s and C-5s.

The DC-8s arrived at Kinshasa airfield that evening and the legionnaires were greeted with the news that they were to emplane almost at once in four C-130 Hercules and two C-160 Transall aircraft of the Zairian air force to fly some 1,240 miles (2,000km) to Kolwezi. Their task was to carry out a "humanitarian combat mission" to rescue all civilians, of whatever race or colour, trapped in and around Kolwezi. Little firm information could be given on the situation in Kolwezi. Few of the men had ever jumped from C-130s and all would have to use American T-10 parachutes which they were not used to. The jump would be from an altitude of 650ft (200m).

The men of 2^{e}REP worked through the night to get organised, and were then piled somewhat haphazardly into the aircraft. The situation was exacerbated when a C-160 blew a tyre on take-off and the legionnaires were taken out of that aircraft and told to push their way into the five remaining machines. With 80 paratroops stuffed into an aircraft designed to take 66, carrying strange parachutes, after a long journey from Corsica and having had no sleep for 48 hours, plus a bumpy four-hour flight to the jump point, the situation seemed ripe for disaster. However, due to the innate good sense of the legionnaires and their sound training, all went smoothly somehow. ▶

Left: Legionnaires of 2^e REP move through the scrub near Kolwezi looking for "Tigers" or their unfortunate European victims.

▶ The drop, 2^{e}REP's first operational jump since Dien Bien Phu, was successful, even though the pilot dropped them directly onto the objective rather than the previously selected DZ some 1,100 yards (1,000m) distant. The men had no heavy weapons, but even though there was no immediate response to their arrival they dug in rapidly. 1^e Cie occupied the Lycee John Paul XXIII, 2^e Cie the hospital and a workshop, and 3^e Cie the Hotel Impala and an overpass.

The night passed with sporadic action and early the next morning the four C-130s and a lone C-160 arrived overhead with further men from the regiment. The commanding officer decided that the situation did not warrant the risk of a night jump and sent the aircraft off to nearby Lubumbashi. They returned at dawn and dropped the men and equipment successfully. During all this the legionnaires got on with the job of bringing order to the city, rescuing prisoners, and dealing (very firmly) with the so-called "Tigers" of the FNLC.

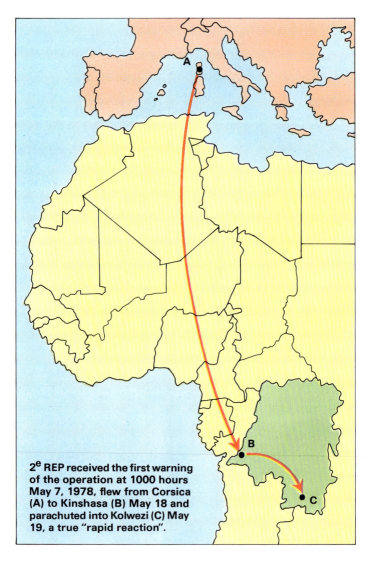

2^e REP received the first warning of the operation at 1000 hours May 7, 1978, flew from Corsica (A) to Kinshasa (B) May 18 and parachuted into Kolwezi (C) May 19, a true "rapid reaction".

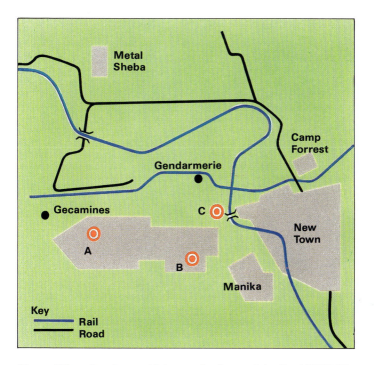

Metal
Sheba

Camp
Forrest

Gendarmerie

Gecamines

C

A

B

New
Town

Manika

Key
—— Rail
—— Road

Above: When they jumped into Kolwezi, 2^e REP deployed quickly to restore order. 2^e Cie occupied the hospital (A), 1^e Cie the Lycee John Paul XXIII (B) and 3^e Cie the Hotel Impala and a road overpass (C). The operation was a great success.

By midday May 20 (two days after the first landing) the situation in Kinshasa was sufficiently under control for 4^e Cie to move out to Metal Shaba, a township some distance to the North, where they bumped a major enemy force which put in a counter-attack against 4^e Cie, using lorryborne infantry supported by two Soviet-built light tanks. They were given short shrift by the Legion.

At first light on May 21 the majority of the regiment's transport arrived from Lubumbashi, followed in the course of the day by the remainder. Mobile at last, the companies spent the next few days scouring the countryside, looking for rebels and their prisoners. Groups of Europeans were found, half-crazed with fear as a result of their harrowing experiences with the "Tigers". A large group of rebels was totally eliminated on May 25. On May 28 2^e REP was ordered to hand over to incoming Belgian, Moroccan and Zairian troops and move to Lubumbashi in preparation for a return to Corsica in C-141s of the USAF.

In this brief operation 2^{e}REP was directly responsible for saving over 3,000 Europeans and many loyal Zairians. Some 300 FNLC "Tigers" were killed and 163 captured, together with vast quantities of arms and ammunition. Five legionnaires were killed in action and 25 wounded, all by small arms fire.

The very rapid move from Corsica to Kinshasa was praiseworthy enough, but the way in which the legionnaires coped with the chaotic arrangements there and their flight to Kolwezi was quite exceptional. The unofficial Legion motto is "Demerdez vous" which literally translated means "Muddle through"; it certainly applied on this occasion.

Paratroops

The French paratroops have probably carried out more operational jumps than any other parachute corps in the world in their campaigns in Indochina, Suez (1956) and Algeria, with others since (e.g., Kolwezi). They have also at times become heavily politicised and for a few days in 1960 the inhabitants of Paris seriously expected *les paras* to drop on the capital to attempt to take over the government.

The French parachute units were among the leading units in the French campaign in Indochina and carried out some 156 operational drops. They harried the Viet Minh ruthlessly, but not without suffering heavy casualties themselves. This culminated in their jump into a small valley in the north-west corner of the country on November 21, 1954, near a small village called Dien Bien Phu. Most parachute units were withdrawn and replaced by heavy infantry once the position had been secured, but when General Giap and the Viet Minh tightened the noose *les paras* returned. Five battalions jumped into the cauldron between March 13 and May 6, some on the day before the garrison fell. The paratroops and the Foreign Legion bore the brunt of the battle and fought with extreme courage—it was just that they were fighting the wrong war in the wrong place.

Following the Indochina ceasefire and the French withdrawal in 1955, the paratroop units went to Algeria, arriving just as the war there started. The paratroops had been staggered by their reverses in Indochina and by their experience in the Viet Minh prisoner-of-war camps, and they set-to to develop an entirely new code for what they saw as a crusade against the Communist-inspired guerrilla threat. They studied Mao Tse-tung's writings avidly and trained their officers and soldiers in new ways.

10th Parachute Division took time off for a brief foray in the frustrating and short-lived Suez ▶

Right: French Army "para" gets away fast from a Puma helicopter. The French were early pioneers of heliborne assault.

Below: Two generations of Vietnam warriors—a French para colonel and Lt Gen Westmoreland, later US commander in Saigon. Note French red beret, para cap-badge and para wings on right breast.

Red beret

Parachute regiment
cap-badge

Ammunition belt for
squad machine gun

Model OF37
hand
grenade

Water
bottle

7.5mm
Model
M1949/56
rifle

19

▶ campaign and then returned to Algeria. In January 1957 this division took over the city of Algiers which was virtually in the control of the FLN and inside two months they totally restored control. Their methods were seriously questioned, however, and there were many allegations of torture. The general frustrations of the French civilians and military in Algeria boiled over in May 1958 in an uprising which eventually led to the return of de Gaulle to the presidency. The paratroops, and in particular their General—Massu— were in the forefront of this affair. They were all also involved in the attempted *putsch* in January 1960, which was very short-lived and ended in ignominious failure.

After the Algerian war the para-troops returned to France, but the French have maintained a strong parachute capability, and have regularly used these excellent troops overseas in pursuit of French diplomatic policies. Units of what is now 11th Parachute Division have served in Zaire, Mauretania, Chad and the Lebanon, among others.

One facet of the French parachute units is the enormous influence they have had on the French Army as a whole in the post-War years. This has been due in large measure to some very powerful characters such as General Jacques Massu and General Marcel Bigeard. The latter entered the Army as a private soldier, was captured as a sergeant in the Maginot Line in 1940 and then escaped to join the Free French in England where he joined the paratroops. He was, without a doubt, one of the finest battalion commanders of his generation in any army, and his reputation was such that his return to Dien Bien Phu had an electrifying effect on the entire garrison. He went on to become a General, and arrived to inspect units by parachute, his arm at the salute as he landed in front of the honour guard.

Organisation

11th Parachute Division is based at Tarbes, although its units are some-what scattered. It is part of the French rapid-intervention force, together with 9th Marine Light Infantry Division, 27th Alpine Division, 6th Light Armoured Division and 4th Airmobile Division. 11th Parachute Division comprises two brigades, with seven battalion-sized parachute units, one of which (1eRPIMa) is under divisional control and has a para-commando/special forces role.

The other six units are: 3, 6 and 8 RPIMa equivalent to the former "colonial" paratroop units); 1 and

Below: French paras deploying from a Puma helicopter. The French have large intervention forces and have not hesitated to use them, particularly in Africa. The paras and the Foreign Legion have spearheaded such missions.

9 RCP (*chasseurs* or light infantry) and 2 REP (the Foreign Legion parachute unit). There are also two independent units: 2nd RPIMa and 13 RDP.

Selection and training

All French paratroops are volunteers and undergo the same sort of selection and training as other parachute forces. The standard of training is high and certain volunteers can go on to join one of the para-commando units (eg, 1^{e}RPIMa).

Weapons and equipment

For many years the French Army has been using the MAS 49/56 7.5mm rifle, but they are now re-equipping with the revolutionary 5.56mm FA MAS, with the parachute units being among the first to receive it. The FA MAS, designed and produced by the St Etienne Arsenal, is of unusual appearance with a carrying-handle which covers almost the entire length of the weapon. With a loaded magazine (25 rounds) the rifle weighs only 8.9lb (4.02kg) and is just 29.8in (757mm) long, all of which make it ideal for paratroopers who require

Above: French Paras in Beirut in 1982. Their ill-conceived mission was to end in tragedy, with many lives lost in a huge terrorist bomb explosion.

a short, light but effective rifle.

The sub-machine gun is still the MAT 9mm Model 49, a robust and reliable weapon with some unusual features. The magazine housing can pivot forward in front of the trigger to enable the magazine to lie along the underside of the barrel, offering obvious economies in space, again, something of great value to a paratrooper. The weapon is completely safe when the magazine is swung forward, but when the magazine is in the "ready-to-fire" position a safety device in the pistol grip operates at all times except when being actually held by the firer.

Uniforms

French paratroops wear standard French Army uniforms. Their parachute status is indicated by their red beret (except for Foreign Legion paras who wear a green beret). Para wings are large and in silver, and are worn on the right breast.

Parachute Regiment

The parachute units of the Indian Army are among the oldest airborne units. The first Indian parachute unit was authorised on May 15, 1941, and by October 1941 50th Indian Parachute Brigade had been formed, comprising 152nd Parachute Battalion (Indian), 151st Parachute Battalion (British) and 153rd Parachute Battalion (Gurkha).

In 1944 it was decided to form a division (44th Indian Parachute Division) and at the same time the formation of the Indian Parachute Regiment as a separate entity was authorised. The partition of the British Indian Empire in 1947 led to the split of the parachute units between India and the newly-created Pakistan. 50th Indian Parachute Brigade was quickly involved in operations in Kashmir 1947-49.

During the 1965 Indo-Pakistan operations a special independent force of commandos was raised and on July 1, 1966, the 9th Parachute Battalion was formed to take on the task, absorbing the smaller commando force in the process. A year later part of 9th Battalion was hived off to form 10th Battalion, each with three company-sized sub-units designated "groups". In 1969 both units added the suffix "commando" to their titles, becoming 9th and 10th Commandos respectively.

Organisation

The Indian Army today has eight parachute battalions, organised into two independent brigades: 50th and 51st. Both brigades have parachute-trained units and sub-units of supporting arms and services—for example, artillery, engineers, signals. 9th and 10th Para Commandos are also still part of the Indian Army order of battle, operating, as all such special forces units do, in an independent role.

Selection and training

All Indian paratroops and para-commandos are volunteers; some enter the regiments direct from civil life, while others transfer in from Regular Army units. There is a probationary period of thirty days when the men undergo various physical and mental tests, during which many are weeded out. Those who pass are sent to the Para-troopers Training School at Agra, where five jumps, including one at night, entitle the trainee to wear the coveted wings and the maroon beret. Paracommandos undergo more specialised training to suit them for their role.

Weapons and equipment

Standard sub-machine gun of India's Army, including the paratroops, is the locally-produced version of the British L2A3 Sterling 9mm. There have been reports that the L34A1 silenced version may be in service in small numbers with the para-commandos. The current rifle is again a locally-produced version of a foreign weapon. This is the Belgian FN 7.62mm FAL, which is made in India at Ishapore. The light machine-gun is the very popular and successful British L4A4, the 7.62mm conversion of the old 0.303in Bren.

Uniforms

The maroon (red) beret has been the headgear of the Indian Parachute Regiment since its inception on March 1, 1945. The capbadge at that time was identical with that of the British Parachute Regiment, except that the word "INDIA" was inscribed at the base of the parachute. This badge was retained through the early years of independence and was changed to the present design—a fully opened parachute on two symbolic wings with an upright bayonet—in 1950. The paracommandos wear the red beret, but their capbadge is a winged dagger above a scroll, all bearing a more than passing resemblance to the capbadge of the British SAS.

Right: This Indian soldier wears the coveted cap badge of one of the oldest para units in any army, raised on May 15, 1941.

Red beret

Regimental
cap-badge

Parachute smock
similar to British
"Dennison" smock

Ammunition
pouch

7.62mm FN FAL
rifle, manufactured
in India

Green denim
trousers

Cloth
puttees

Paratroops

Of all the world's elite paratroop units none has seen so much or so frequent action as those of the Israeli Defence Forces (IDF). Founded in 1948, during the War of Independence, the initial material assets were one dilapidated Curtiss C-46 Commando aircraft and 4,000 second-hand parachutes which had been bought as scrap to make silk shirts! The unit consisted of a mixture of Israeli veterans of the British Army and the Palmach, graduates of a parachute course held in Czechoslovakia, Resistance veterans, ghetto survivors and a number of adventurers.

Training was inadequate and as there were no reserve 'chutes jumps periodically ended in tragedy. The units saw little action in the war and in 1949 a new commander raised standards considerably.

Meanwhile, in the early 1950s frequent infiltration by Arab terrorists led to the formation of a small unit of high quality soldiers for reprisal operations. Named "the 101st", this was very successful, but after a few years it was amalgamated with the Paratroop Unit. After some successful actions in 1954/55 the paratroopers were expanded to brigade strength and

in 1955-56 some very effective reprisal operations were carried out. In the 1956 war the Sinai campaign opened with a drop by a parachute battalion on the Mitla Pass, with the balance of the brigade being responsible for joining up with it by road, an operation which took just 28 hours to achieve. In the battles in and around the Mitla Pass the Israeli paratroops lost 38 dead and over 100 wounded, but the Egyptians lost over 260.

In a second operation a battalion was dropped at At-Tur, on the south-eastern shore of the Gulf of Suez, with the remainder of the brigade again responsible for relieving its own isolated battalion. This done, the whole brigade then moved on to join 9th Infantry ▶

Right: Israeli paratroop on the Entebbe raid stands clear of a deliberate explosion. He carries a Soviet AK-47 rifle, of which the Israelis have vast stocks.

Below: More conventionally clad Israeli paratroops "somewhere in Lebanon". They are armed with the 5.56mm SAR Galil rifle, designed and produced in Israel.

Note:
no helmet

Israeli
webbing
equipment

Two magazines
strapped back-to-
back for quick
change in action

Captured
Soviet AK-47
assault
rifle

Magazine
pouch

Water
bottle

Israeli
combat
uniform

▶ Brigade in the capture of Sharm-el-Sheikh.

After more years of reprisal raids the Paratroops played a leading role in the 1967 Six-Day War. They were involved in operations at Gaza and on the Suez Canal, but their greatest moment came when they achieved the goal of every Israeli by recapturing the Old City of Jerusalem on June 7, 1967. This battle involved taking great care to ensure that there was no damage to the holiest shrines of three major religions, which inevitably meant that the paratroops took more casualties than normal.

After the war more raids were undertaken, including those against the PLO HQ in Jordan (March 21, 1968, 250 enemy killed), the capture and return to Israel of a complete Soviet radar installation (December 23, 1969), the destruction of Arab aircraft at Beirut airport (December 12, 1968) and the rescue of hostages in a hijacked Sabena aircraft at Lod Airport (May 12, 1972).

In the Yom Kippur war the paratroopers did not undertake any parachute operations, but were involved in some desperate fighting, first to hold back the Egyptian attack and then to turn the tables by both containing enemy troops on the west bank of the canal and by crossing the canal itself into Egyptian home territory.

In July 1976 the paratroops provided the men for the raid on Entebbe where they lost their commanding officer—Lieutenant Colonel "Yoni" Netanyahu, leading his men, as always, from the front. Since then the paratroops have been involved in more fighting, particularly in the Lebanon.

Organisation

There are five parachute brigades in the IDF. Two of these are normally at, or very near, full strength; one is well above 50 per cent; and two are at cadre strength. The IDF's very efficient call-out and training system ensures that units depending upon reservists for achieving war strength are reinforced very quickly, indeed.

Below: Paratroops are inherently flexible. These Israeli paras are disembarking from a tank-landing ship mounted in M113 armoured personnel carriers on an operation in the Lebanon.

Right: Israeli paratroops on parade; note the red berets and parachute wings on the left breast. The corporal nearest the camera carries an UZI 9mm SMG, widely used by parachute forces.

Selection and training

All fit males in Israel must perform three years of military service, and all may volunteer for the parachute troops. Selection and training are rigorous, and emphasise practical military skills such as weapon training, demolitions, covert cross-border operations and field medicine. The physical requirements are very tough. All must obviously qualify as parachutists and many then go on to specialise in HALO techniques. Night operations and helicopter assault are regularly practised. ▶

Right: Israeli paratrooper at the ready. He carries the 7.62mm ARM Galil assault rifle. This version has a carrying-handle, a bipod (folded under the barrel), and a folding stock.

▶ Weapons and equipment

Like other units of the IDF the paratroops use Israeli weapons and equipment wherever possible, but supplemented with either purchased items of Western origin or captured items (usually, but not always, of Eastern origin). Parachutes are American, but small arms are Israeli. For many years the Israeli paratroops have used the Uzi sub-machine gun, but this is now being replaced by the Galil SAR rifle, an Israeli-designed and produced 5.56mm weapon with a 35-round magazine. An extremely robust and reliable weapon, the Galil incorporates the lessons learned in Israel's continuous conflicts of the past 35 years. Its advantages to the paratroops, in comparison with the Uzi, are that it provides greater range, hitting power and penetration.

Uniforms

IDF paratroopers wear standard Israeli uniforms and helmets. The customary parachutist's red beret is worn when the glassfibre combat helmet is not required. The parachutist's badge is in silver and is worn on the left breast above campaign medals.

269 Counterterrorist Unit

The existence of a special group within the IDF parachute troops has been reported from time to time. Designated 269 Counterterrorist Unit this is said to be the unit which provided the men for the raid on Entebbe. If these reports are correct it can be presumed that the unit is a specially trained and equipped group at a high state of readiness, and akin to West Germany's GSG 9 in function.

Right: Israeli frogman on the shoreline aims his Galil assault rifle, resting the bipod on a rock to steady his aim. The Galil is modelled in some respects on the Soviet AK-47 series, but also incorporates the lessons of 50 years of warfare in Israel.

Operation Jonathan Entebbe Rescue 3/4 July 1976

At 0900 hours June 27, 1976, Air France flight AF 139 left Tel Aviv airport en route for Paris. The A-300 Airbus aircraft staged through Athens and it was on the second leg of its flight when, at 1210 hours, it was skyjacked by seven Palestinian terrorists led by a German called Boese. The pilot succeeded in pressing the "hijack button" as he turned for Benghazi, where, after a 6½ hour delay, the plane was refuelled; it then flew on to the terrorists' destination—Entebbe in Uganda, which was under the erratic rule of "Field Marshal" Idi Amin Dada.

Amin endeavoured to maintain a neutral posture, but covertly he supported the terrorists in their demands that unless Palestinian prisoners held in a number of countries were released the hostages would be shot at 1200 hours on July 1. Ugandan troops were deployed at Entebbe airport, supposedly to "keep the peace", but they were in fact assisting in guarding the hostages. Amin even visited the hostages and after he had left the Israelis and Jews of other nationalities were segregated, although the entire Air France aircrew insisted on joining them.

On the morning of July 1 the Isaelis, playing for time, announced that they were willing to consider the release of Palestinian prisoners. The hijackers, increasingly confident of eventual success, responded by extending their deadline by three days. They also released all the non-Jewish hostages, who were flown to Paris, where they were given detailed debriefing by French and Israeli intelligence.

The Israeli planners had many problems. The first clearly was shortage of time: time to achieve something before the terrorists killed any of their hostages and time to set up a rescue attempt. The second was to find out just where the hostages were being held and under what conditions. Third, there was the problem of ▶

getting a rescue force all the way to Entebbe and back with the rescued hostages. Fourth, there was the problem of what to do with the non-Jewish hostages.

Fortunately, the problems re-

Above: A scene from the EMI film "Operation Thunderbolt" showing the staff planners with a detailed model of the airfield at Entebbe. (No photographs of the rescue were released.)

► solved themselves one after another. The Kenya government agreed to the use of Nairobi airport, and a coup in Sudan resulted in the closure of all but one of that country's air control radars. Intelligence on Entebbe Airport and the local situation began to be processed in, aided considerably by the debriefing of the released non-Jewish hostages. This also removed the problem of consulting foreign governments, except that of France who remained involved not only because it had been an Air France airliner that was hijacked in the first place, but also because the courageous crew insisted on staying with the Jewish hostages.

The Rescue

Lieutenant-General Mordecai Gur, Israeli chief-of-staff, considered that a raid on the airport was feasible and at 0730 hours on July 3 Prime Minister Rabin reviewed all the facts and then gave the political go-ahead for the operation. Later that morning a full-scale dress rehearsal was held in northern Israel. The force, commanded by Brigadier-General Dan Shomron, aged 48, performed well in an attack on a dummy layout manned by Israeli troops, and all seemed to augur well for the real thing, which was scheduled for the next day. The dress rehearsal lasted just 55 minutes from the time the aircraft

EMI

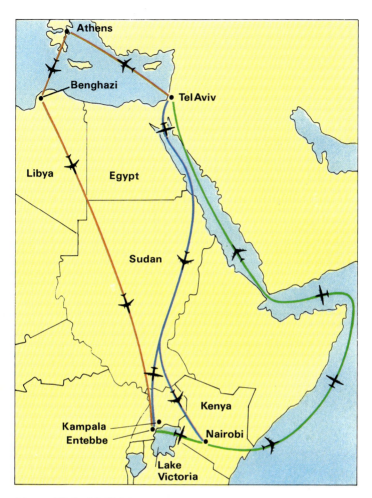

Above: Flight AF 139 (red) was hijacked on leaving Athens and taken via Benghazi to Entebbe. The rescuers flew in two groups (blue). Four C-130s refuelled at Eilat and then flew down the Red Sea, along the Sudan-Ethiopia border and into Entebbe. The other group (two Boeing 707s) followed, one circling Entebbe as a command post, the other a medical aircraft going to Nairobi. The rescuers returned (green) via Nairobi to a heroes' welcome.

Left: Another scene from the film, with Israeli paratroops relaxing in the hold of a C-130 transport aircraft on the long, hazardous flight to Entebbe.

landed to the time they took off again. The force to enter the airport terminal and rescue the hostages was to be led by Lieutenant-Colonel Jonathan Netanyahu, known throughout the Israeli Army as "Yoni". Shomron, an experienced paratrooper, had led several penetration raids into Egypt, and had been commanding officer of the first infantry battalion to reach the Suez Canal in the 1967 Arab-Israeli War. Netanyahu was nine years younger and had already been decorated for bravery, and was a very popular officer.

At 1600 hours that afternoon (July 3), only two hours after the full Israeli cabinet had been made aware of the "go" decision, four ▶

Above: Israeli paratroops pour into the Entebbe airport building where the hostages are being held (a filmed reconstruction).

▶ C-130 Hercules aircraft of the Israeli Air Force took off for the long flight to Entebbe. The route took them down the middle of the Red Sea at high altitude in the hope that Saudi Arabian radars would treat them as unscheduled civil flights. There was, in fact, no response, so they were able to turn and fly down the Sudan-Ethiopia border and into Uganda.

Two Boeing 707s were also involved, leaving two hours after the slower C-130s. One was a flying command-post fitted with special communications; it caught up with the four C-130s near Entebbe and remained in the area throughout the operation with Major Generals Benny Peled and Yekutiel Adam aboard. The other 707, fitted out as an emergency hospital, went straight to Nairobi, arriving just before midnight; it then waited, its medical staff ready for any wounded from the operation across the border in Uganda.

The four C-130s arrived at Entebbe without incident and landed at precisely 0001 hours. The first aircraft landed close to the control-tower disgorging its paratroops in a Mercedes car and three Land Rovers while still moving. The men charged into the tower and succeeded in preventing the controllers from switching off the landing lights; even so, emergency lights were deployed, just in case. These were not needed and the second and third aircraft taxied up to the terminal where the hostages were being held and discharged their paratroopers straight into action. The fourth C-130 joined the first near the control tower.

The main Israeli squad brushed aside the slight and ineffective resistance from the Ugandan Army guards, killing some twenty in the process, and charged into the terminal building. The second group went off to destroy as many as possible of the Ugandan Air Force MiG-15, -17 and -21 jet fighters standing on the runway; this served both to prevent pursuit when the raiders took off again and also as a noisy and obvious diversion. The third group went to the perimeter to cover the approach road since it was known that the Ugandan Army had a number of Soviet-built T-54 tanks and Czech OT-64 armoured personnel carriers some 20 miles (32km) away in the capital, Kampala. Had this force appeared it could have had a major effect as the Israelis had no heavy weapons; fortunately, nothing happened. The fourth group was made up of 33 doctors who, being Israelis, were also well-trained soldiers and brought down covering fire from the area of the C-130s.

With Shomron in control in the tower and satisfied that the first phase had been successful it was now "Yoni" Netanyahu's turn to lead the crucial assault on the terminal building to rescue the hostages. The terrorist leader, Wilfried Boese, behaved with surprising indecision, first aiming at the hostages and then changing his mind, going outside, loosing off a few rounds at the Israelis and then heading back for the lounge; as he returned he was shot and killed. His fellow German, Gabrielle Tiedemann, was also killed outside the building.

The Israeli soldiers rushed into the lounge where the hostages were being held, shouting at everyone to get down on the floor; in the confusion three of the hostages were shot by stray bullets, an almost inevitable consequence in such a situation. While some of the soldiers rushed upstairs to kill the two terrorists remaining there, the hostages were shepherded out to the waiting C-130s. At this point "Yoni" Netanyahu emerged from the terminal to supervise the loading and was killed by one shot from a Ugandan solider in a nearby building, a sad loss.

At 0045 hours the defensive outposts were called in as the first C-130 roared off into the night with its load of rescued hostages on their way to Nairobi, with the fourth and last leaving at 0054.

The whole operation had taken just 53 minutes, two minutes less than the rehearsal.

The Israelis lost Colonel Netanyahu killed and three men wounded. Three hostages were killed in the rescue, while a fourth, Mrs Dora Bloch, who had been taken off to a local hospital earlier, was murdered by the Ugandans in revenge for the raid.

The whole operation was a brilliant success, mounted at short notice and in a most unexpected direction. It confirmed the Israeli reputation for quick and determined "ad hoc" actions, conducted with great dedication and skill. The Ugandans could not be described as substantial foes, but the terrorists had obviously been trained for their task. Interestingly, it later became known that Colonel Ulrich Wegener of GSG 9 was with the Israelis on the operation, possibly because of the known presence of the two Germans with the terrorists.

Below: Israeli rescuer in the assault on the Entebbe airport building. He is armed with a 9mm UZI sub-machine gun, standard issue to all Israeli forces.

EMI

Alpine Troops

The major land threat to Italy comes from the North and Northeast, and virtually the whole of this strategically critical region is mountainous. For this reason the Italian Army has long maintained its units of crack mountain troops—the famous Alpini. There are five mountain brigades (*brigata alpina*): Taurinese, Orobica, Tridentia, Cadore and Julia. These serve in three army corps: III Corps (HQ at Milan) includes one mountain brigade; IV Corps (Bolzano) is responsible for the defence of the crucial Brenner Pass and has three mountain brigades; and V Corps (Vittorio Veneto) is responsible for the north-eastern border with Austria and Jugoslavia, and has one mountain brigade; finally, one Alpini battalion is permanently assigned to the Allied Command Europe Mobile Force (Land).

Mountain brigades' major combat elements are one mountain infantry regiment of three or four Alpini battalions and an independent APC

company, and an Alpini artillery regiment with three battalions of 105mm pack-howitzers and one battalion of 155mm towed howitzers. There are also a fortress battalion, a parachute-ski platoon, a carabinieri platoon, a signal company and an engineer company. Last, but by no means least, is the logistics regiment, whose basic means of transportation is mules.

The Italian Army is due to decrease in size in the near future to reduce personnel costs and increase the amount of finance available for equipment. Although the number of brigades is due to reduce from 36 to 24 it is significant that there is to be no reduction in either the Alpine or parachute brigades. ▶

Below: Light machine gun team of an Alpini unit. Their weapon is the 7.62mm MG42/59 made in Italy by Beretta under licence from Rheinmetall. Note national flash on soldiers' left shoulder.

▶ Selection and training

The 2nd Alpine Regiment is responsible for basic training and there is also an Alpine warfare school. All soldiers in the mountain brigades must be trained in mountain warfare, which requires a very high standard of fitness and determination. The Italian Army as a whole has a major training problem, however, because it is made up of conscripts who serve only for twelve months, of which the first three are devoted to basic training. Add in specialist training and there is not much time left for service with a combat unit.

Weapons and equipment

Standard weapon of the Alpini soldier is currently the Beretta BM59 Mark Ital TA 7.62mm rifle (TA = Truppe Alpini). This weapon is an Italian development of the US Garand M1 0.30in rifle. The basic rifle—the BM59 Mark Ital—weighs 10lb (4.6kg) and has an effective range of 656 yards (600m). The Mark Ital TA has a tubular metal folding butt, a pistol grip and a

Right: Alpini soldier in a good firing position with his MILAN anti-tank missile. Note the snow shoe to the left of the tree; despite the legends these are of use only for short distances.

Below: Italian Alpini being towed by a Norwegian Army oversnow vehicle on an Allied Mobile Force (Land) (AMF(L)) exercise in Norway. The AMF(L) is a vital NATO force under SACEUR's direct command in peace and would be first to deploy in a crisis.

special winter trigger to enable it to be fired when wearing gloves. Standard SMG is the 9mm Model 38/49 Beretta, a sturdy and reliable weapon, although the design is a development of a weapon first produced in 1938.

One item, designed for the Alpini artillery, which has become world famous, is the Oto Melara 105mm Model 56 pack-howitzer. This gun can be broken down into eleven sections for transportation by pack-mules. It has a range of 11,565 yards (10,575m) and over 2,400 have been sold to some 25 armies.

Uniform

The most instantly recognisable feature of Alpini dress is the famous grey-green felt mountain-eers' hat, with a black eagle feather and red pompom on the left-hand side. The cap badge is of black metal and depicts an eagle above a light-infantry bugle containing the regimental number. The eagle feather and pompom are also worn on the steel helmet. The Alpini collar-patch is green. In parade dress the officers wear the tra-ditional blue sash.

There are various types of combat dress, varying from standard com-bat uniform to full mountain gear of white hooded overall and trousers with a white-covered steel helmet.

San Marco Marines

The Multinational peace-keeping force in the Lebanon from 1982 to 1984 was not, in general terms, a great success, and certainly failed to fulfil its political aims. The individual military contingents did, however, conduct themselves well and one in particular that earned considerable praise was that from Italy, which was provided by the San Marco battalion of the Italian Marines, one of the elite units of the Italian Armed Forces.

The San Marco battalion is the major combat element of the 1,000 strong Italian Marines, and its men are trained in the full range of marine duties, especially amphibious warfare. They are also all parachute trained. Their mission is to provide an amphibious capability (albeit, in view of their size, a limited one) in support of the Italian and NATO fleets in the Mediterranean.

Organisation

The San Marco battalion is divided into three components: the Operational Group of four companies; the Logistics Group and the Training Group. Battalion sea transport is provided by two ex-USN Landing Ships Tank (LST), the *Caorle* (ex-USS *York County*) and the *Grado* (ex-USS *De Soto County*). So important and successful is the battalion, however, that the Italian Navy is planning under the 1975 Naval Law to build a new ship, a Landing Platform Dock (LPD) of 7,667 tons, which will have a large flight-deck for helicopters as well as a tank/vehicle deck and roll-on/roll-off facilities. Some doubts about the need for such a specialised and expensive ship have been removed by the San Marco deployment to Lebanon, and it will now be commissioned by the end of 1967.

Fighting vehicles of the battalion ▶

Above: San Marco marines going ashore in MTP 9733, an Italian-built landing-craft. The San Marco battalion is Italy's only marine unit.

Below: San Marco marines storm ashore under the setting sun. Their weapons are the latest 5.56mm Beretta SC70 assault rifles with tubular folding butts.

BIGHI (SMM – UDAP)

Above: A squad of San Marco marines ready for an operation. Note the unique camouflage colours on the combat uniforms.

Below: 81mm mortar team leads a beach landing from LCVPs. The San Marco use few specialised weapons (see text).

include the M113A1 armoured personnel carrier, 10 LVTP-7 amphibious landing vehicles and 30 VCC-1, an Italian-produced improved version of the M113, which it is replacing.

Weapons and equipment

The San Marco battalion uses the same weapons as other Italian units in the main, for example, 7.62mm Beretta BM 59 Mark Ital (see Alpini entry). However, limited issues have been made of a new rifle, the 5.56mm AR70/223 Beretta. This appears in two versions: the standard with a solid butt, and the SC70 with a folding butt. This is a very neat and simple weapon, which is light and easy to handle.

A short-barelled version is also being tested, ideal for use by special forces. All are slightly heavier than the M16A1, the standard by which all modern rifles are judged, but offer some improvements in reliability and ease of maintenance.

Uniform

San Marco marines wear the usual, and easily recognisable, Italian camouflage suit, and the steel helmet whose design has not changed in forty years. A black beret is worn and the San Marco lion badge, gold on a red backing, is worn on the right sleeve cuff.

In combat dress the San Marco marines dress as soldiers, but in parade order they wear naval uniform, with the embellishment of the San Marco lion badge, worn by officers on the left breast above the medal ribbons and by marines on the tunic shirt cuffs. This curious mixing of army and naval uniforms is unique.

Special Forces

A company of paratroopers was raised in 1963 and, having quickly proved its value, this has been expanded over the years until today there are three battalions of commando/paratroops, now retitled the Jordanian Special Forces. These units have taken part in numerous operations in the various Middle East wars, and have also been heavily involved during peacetime in keeping control of their troubled country. They played a leading part in the operations to suppress and finally expel the Palestine Liberation Army (PLO) commandos in 1970-71, and also retook the Inter-Continental Hotel in Amman in 1976.

Such is the reputation of the Special Forces that in 1983 the US military authorities suggested that the force be expanded to two-brigade size and used to help cope with the security problems in the Persian Gulf. This somewhat naive proposal was very complimentary to the Jordanian Special Forces, but has fortunately been dropped, as its effect both internationally and domestically within Jordan would be catastrophic.

Organisation

The three commando/paratroop battalions are organised on standard Jordanian Army lines with three companies, each of three platoons. Battalions are approximately 500 strong.

Selection and training

Members of the Jordanian Special Forces are all volunteers. They must be Bedouins with personal tribal links to King Hussein, and a proven record of undoubted loyalty. Training is the toughest in an army noted for its high standards and all men are trained in parachute, guerrilla and sabotage techniques.

Weapons and equipment

The three Special Forces battalions are equipped as light infantry, with weapons such as Dragon anti-tank guided missiles, 106mm recoilless rifles, mortars and small arms (M16 rifle, M60 MG, etc). Land transport is based on the usual jeeps and trucks. Air mobility is provided by the Royal Jordanian Air Force whose transport fleet includes: 15 Alouette III and two S-76 helicopters (with four more S-76 on order), three C-130 Hercules, and four Casa C-212 Aviocars.

Uniform

As with the rest of the army, the Jordanian Special Forces' uniform shows both British and United States' influence. US-style leaf-pattern camouflage suits are worn and most items of personal equipment are of US origin. Parachute wings are worn on the left breast and the major visible mark is the maroon beret, but worn with the standard national cap-badge. The Special Forces' badge is a white bayonet surrounded by symbolic yellow wings and surmounted by a Hashemite crown; this is backed by a maroon shield and worn on the right upper sleeve.

Right and below: Members of Jordan's elite Special Forces formation, with M16 rifle and US-style combat dress. Jordan's Army is one of the best in the Middle East. Jordan Special Forces were proposed by the Pentagon as the basis for a "fire-brigade" force in the Middle East.

Helmet with
camouflage cover

US Army temperate
climate camouflaged
combat uniform

5.56mm
M16A1 rifle

Ammunition
pouches

M61 delay
fragmentation
grenade

Respiration
bag

43

Special Forces

The forces of the Democratic Republic of Korea (North) invaded the Republic of Korea (South) (ROK) on June 25, 1950. The resulting war pulled in the Republic of China on the side of the North, and 16 nations (including the USA) on the ROK side. An armistice (not a peace treaty) was signed on July 27, 1953, and an uneasy "peace" has continued since.

Currently stationed in South Korea is the United States 8th Army, comprising 2nd Infantry Division, 19th Support Command, at least one wing of the USAF and numerous supporting units. The ROK Army comprises five corps, with one mechanised and 20 infantry divisions, two armoured brigades and a host of minor units. It also includes seven Special Forces brigades.

In contrast, the army of North Korea comprises eight corps, with two tank divisions, three motorised infantry divisions, 35 infantry divisions and the usual supporting elements. Included in these massive forces in the North are no fewer than 22 Special Forces (or commando) brigades. The North Koreans have built up sufficient forces in the central part of their territory to launch a deep and sudden attack, without help from either the USSR or PRC, which would threaten Seoul, only some 28 miles (45km) south of the DMZ. Such an attack could be facilitated by the tunnels which have been dug from time to time. One (the third) was discovered on December 27, 1978, and was 6.6ft (2m) square, quite large enough for small vehicles and light ▶

Above: All members of the South Korean Special Forces must reach black belt standard in Tae-Kwon-Do or a similar martial art; there is 4-5 hours practice daily.

Below: Soldiers of a Special Forces unit coming ashore in an inflatable boat. Rifles are US M16A1 5.56mm, but its successor will be a Korean design.

45

▶ guns. The Communist Special Forces brigades could use such tunnels or deploy by air or sea.

The ROK has seven Special Forces brigades organised on the same lines as US Special Forces groups, with whom there is a close working relationship. The battalions of these brigades are often used in the Ranger role for the destruction of tactical targets. These ROK Special Forces units are capable of using either continuous guerrilla operations from bases within enemy territory, or carrying out single operations from bases within friendly territory. The usual allocation of the Special Forces is one battalion to each army corps.

Selection and training

Following the usual physical and psychological tests, the volunteer undergoes a hard training course which includes weapon handling skills to a very high standard and parachute training. All ROK Special Forces troops must also reach black belt standard in Tae-Kwon-Do or a similar martial art, and when not on operations some four to five hours a day are spent in practice of such arts.

Weapons and equipment

Standard sub machine-gun in use by the Korean special forces is the US-supplied 0.45 M3A1, although this must be due for replacement by a more modern and effective weapon in the near future. The rifle of the South Korean Army is the M16A1, locally manufactured, and the squad machine-gun is the 7.62mm M60. The South Koreans are, however, taking steps to become more independent in the arms field—they have recently produced a prototype of their first ever tank design—and can therefore be considered likely to produce their own small arms, also.

Uniform

Normal uniform is a camouflage combat suit. The Special Forces distinguishing mark is a black beret with the SF badge in silver. Weapons and personal equipment are all of US origin. Pocket patches are sometimes worn, with different badges for each SF brigade.

Below: Special Forces troops on winter warfare training, firing M16A1 rifles from rests made from ski sticks. Korean winters are very severe, as the UN forces found out in 1950 to 1953.

Right: Special Forces troops climb a rock face, having come ashore from canoes. Weapon is 9mm Mini UZI SMG. Israeli-designed for police and special forces, it weighs 5.9lb (2.7kg).

Selous Scouts

It is, perhaps, one of the signs of modern life that memories are short and that wars of five years ago become as much as part of history as World War II. Thus, the Rhodesian War which ended in 1980 and those who took part in it are now all but forgotten by the world at large. Following Ian Smith's unilaterial declaration of independence (UDI) in November 1965 there was sporadic guerrilla activity, but in 1973 this developed into a major campaign, strengthened when the Portuguese were forced out of Mozambique in 1974.

The war was expensive in lives on both sides. Inside Rhodesia some 3,244 people were killed in 1976 (234 security forces, 1,904 guerrillas, 66 white civilians and 1,040 black civilians), and 3,067 in 1977 (197 security forces, 1,759 guerrillas, 56 white and 1,055 black civilians).

Spearheading the ground war was one of the more famous and successful special forces units of recent times—the Selous Scouts—who claimed more terrorists killed than the rest of the Rhodesian Army put together. This force originated in 1974 as the Tracker Combat Unit, but was subsequently redesignated the Selous Scouts in memory of Frederick Selous, a friend of Cecil Rhodes, who helped in the opening up to white colonisation much of what later became Rhodesia.

The primary role of the Selous Scouts was in gaining intelligence through deep penetration patrols and tracking, but they did not avoid combat when the opportunity arose.

Organisation

The Selous Scouts numbered about 700 at the height of the war, and were recruited from all races in the country. The commanding officer was Colonel Reid-Daly, who had served with the Rhodesian SAS in Malaya, and all offficers were white, including a few from the UK and USA. The soldiers were initially mostly white, but as the war progressed blacks became the majority group.

The Selous Scouts worked in "sticks" of 4 or 5 men, who undertook self-contained operations for protracted periods. They frequently disguised themselves as guerrilla groups, or even, in the case of the whites, as East German advisers to the ZIPRA and ZANLA forces.

Selection and training

Selection and training were tough, with great emphasis placed upon the ability to survive in small, isolated groups in the bush. Most officers and men came from the Rhodesian countryside and were therefore used to hunting and tracking wild game. With further training and experience they became masters at tracking guerrillas.

All were qualified parachutists, using the American T10 parachute. Most drops were made from antiquated, but still effective, DC-3 Dakota aircraft from a height of 500ft (152m), the low height minimising descent times (about 20 seconds). Some men were trained in HALO techniques, although these were rarely utilised on operations.

Weapons and equipment

Although the Rhodesians managed to obtain arms and equipment despite the various trade embargoes, they frequently had to make do with less than the ideal and simply use whatever was available. Thus, the Selous Scouts' main weapon was the Fabrique Nationale FAL 7.62mm rifle, which was rather heavy and large for their requirements; the US M16 or the Soviet AK-47 would have been much more suitable, and, in fact, some of the latter were carried following their capture from guerrillas.

▶

Right: Soldier of the elite Selous Scouts during a counter-terrorist operation. One of the toughest elite units of recent times, the Scouts were effective but often controversial.

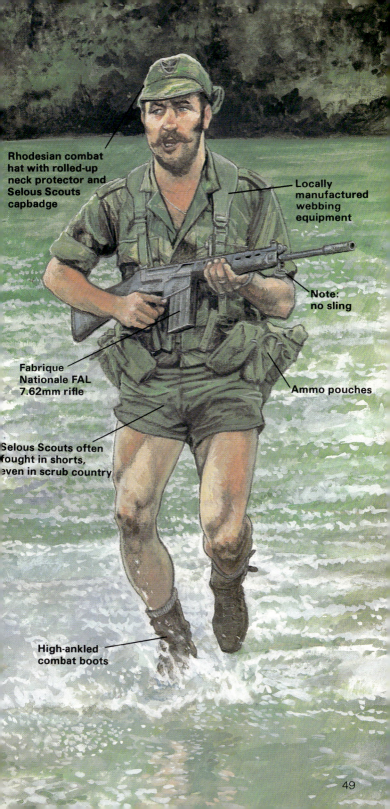

Rhodesian combat hat with rolled-up neck protector and Selous Scouts capbadge

Locally manufactured webbing equipment

Note: no sling

Fabrique Nationale FAL 7.62mm rifle

Ammo pouches

Selous Scouts often fought in shorts, even in scrub country

High-ankled combat boots

49

▶ Uniform

Selous Scouts were probably allowed more latitude in dress than any equivalent military group in any contemporary army. Officially the combat dress was the Rhodesian Army camouflaged uniform with the peaked, camouflaged hat, and attached neckflap. Brown leather boots and webbing anklets were also part of this outfit. In practice the men frequently wore only khaki shorts and track shoes, either with or without a khaki T-shirt and cap. The only equipment regularly carried was a rifle and a water-bottle on a sling. Obviously, such an outfit was used only for short-range operations of limited duration, and heavier clothing, rations and ammunition were held in rucksacks at a patrol base.

In formal dress the Selous Scouts' distinguishing mark was a sand-colored beret, similar to that worn by the SAS.

Other Rhodesian Special Forces

To Rhodesia belongs the distinction of raising the first SAS unit outside the British Army. To help deal with the Malayan Emergency the British raised the Malayan Scouts (SAS) in 1950, and the Rhodesians were asked to assist. This they readily agreed to do, and from some 1,000 volunteers were selected enough suitable officers and men to form what became C Squadron of the Malayan Scouts (SAS).

The squadron returned to Rhodesia where it continued as C Squadron, Rhodesian SAS. The unit went through a low period in the early 1960s, especially after the collapse of the short-lived Federation of Rhodesia and Nyasaland in 1963, and at one point it was down to a few officers and some 24 men.

From 1964 C Squadron's role gradually expanded and its numbers increased. Portugal was fighting guerrilla wars in Angola and Mozambique at the time and periodically C Squadron joined in. Some men operated with the Portuguese Army in Angola in 1967, and from 1970 to 1974 there were regular operations in Mozambique to the east and north.

Gradually, however, the guerrilla assault on Rhodesia itself began to build up and the squadron's role became more involved with its own national problems. During its operations C Squadron specialised in surprise attacks against guerrilla bases in Rhodesia, Zambia and Mozambique. Such raids were frequently mounted from the air, although canoes and boats were sometimes used, besides approaches on foot.

By 1977 the size of the squadron had grown to about 250, and in 1978 it was redesignated the Rhodesian Special Air Service Regiment. It was still in existence at the time of the handover of power to Robert Mugabe's government (of what is now called Zimbabwe).

Selection and training

Unlike other Special Forces units in Rhodesia the SAS remained all-white throughout. Its selection criteria remained very high at all times, even in the period of rapid expansion following UDI. The selection course was rigorous in the extreme. The volunteers were greeted by a "sickener" period of 36 to 48 hours continuous and strenuous activity in which they were allowed no sleep. This was followed immediately by a 20 mile (32km) endurance march carrying a rifle, ammunition and a 40lb (18kg) pack. Not surprisingly this tended to weed out all but the most highly motivated.

Training included canoeing, Scuba diving and parachuting, both static-line and free-fall. Forty per cent went on to qualify in HALO techniques, which were used frequently on operations, especially at night. The men who went through all this were still not "badged" to SAS until they had completed several live operations and had satisfied all concerned that they fully merited entry to such an exclusive unit.

The other Special Forces unit was Gray's Scouts, a unique unit of some 200 men. They were horse-mounted infantry (a form of modern dragoons) who undertook patrols and tracking operations.

Aftermath

The Selous Scouts and Rhodesian SAS were among the most effective units in the guerrilla war. They were therefore especially feared and loathed by the enemy and were made the objects of a virulent hate campaign in the world's Press. As a result, the great majority of whites in the two units left the country when Mugabe came to power, many of them reputedly moving to South Africa to continue their fight against the guerrillas from there. As to the black members of the Selous Scouts, their fate is not clear.

Below: Rhodesian SAS trooper calls in air support during a cross-border operation. The Rhodesian SAS was raised to help the British in Malaya in 1950-53 and became one of the most effective units in Rhodesia's long, last war.

Radio antenna

amouflage
carf worn
s sweat band

Alouette
helicopter

dio
ndset

7.62mm FN
FAL rifle

ter
ttle

Ammunition
pouches

Reconnaissance Commandos

As the military threat to the Republic of South Africa (RSA) has gathered strength over the past decade, the army of that country has had to gird itself for a lengthy campaign against a relentless, but by no means unbeatable, foe. Despite the recent accord with Mozambique the conflict will go on for years to come as the USSR, and their Cuban clients, fan the flames. The various external and internal operations have inevitably forced the South African Defence Forces to develop a number of special units, including the 32nd Battalion, which is composed almost entirely of disaffected Angolans, but the elite is undoubtedly the Reconnaissance Commando, popularly known as the "Recce Commandos" or just "Recces". (Commando is, of course, an honourable title in South African history, having been used to designate similar units in the Boer War against the British at the start of the Century.)

The primary "Recce" mission is to operate deep inside enemy territory, gaining information and tracking enemy units. This is a similar task to that of the erstwhile Selous Scouts of the Rhodesian Army, and it could well be that a number of former members of that outfit have joined South Africa's "Recces".

All "Recce" soldiers are trained parachutists, qualifying in both static and free-fall techniques, with many capable of HALO insertion. A number also receive training in seaborne operations, including underwater swimming. Tracking and survival in the bush are obviously essential, together with the usual special forces skills in using explosives, radios, enemy weapons, and in unarmed combat. They also qualify as paramedics.

Selection and training

Selection courses for the Recce Commandos are of 42 weeks duration and are held twice a year. Unlike many other such courses they are open not only to volunteers from the South African army, but from the navy and air force as well. The average age of those attending the course is 19, and only about 6 to 10 per cent are ultimately successful. Medical and psychological tests are necessary preliminaries to attending the selection course, as is the physical test which includes: covering 20 miles (32km) in 6 hours, carrying full equipment, FN FAL rifle and a 70lb (32kg) sand-bay; various physical exercises (e.g. 40 push-ups) within a specified time, and timed runs; swimming free-style for 50 yards (46m).

The selection course takes place in Zululand, and is carried out in an operational environment. The standards set are extremely tough, and great emphasis is placed on pushing the volunteers to the limit. One of the final tests, for example, is to make the men spend one or two nights alone in the bush, with just a rifle and some ammunition to protect themselves from wild animals. The result of all this is to produce a very highly skilled, capable, and motivated soldier, who is thoroughly at home in the combat environment of today's southern Africa, either on his own or as a member of a group.

Weapons and equipment

Standard small-arms are used, such as the FN 7.62mm FAL rifle (sometimes with a folding stock) and the FN MAG light machine-gun. Many soldiers carry fighting knives.

Uniform

Recce commandos wear standard South African combat dress of sand-coloured jacket and slacks, with high-ankled boots and a floppy "jungle-hat". The usual heavy canvas web equipment is also worn. In the field the soldiers, all of whom are white, use black camouflage cream to disguise their race at a distance.

Right: South African elite "Recce" on a punitive mission leaves a burning village that has been a terrorist haven.

Combat hat

Blackened face

Light khaki combat uniform

Green canvas webbing equipment

Combat knife

Ammunition pouches

Water bottle

7.62mm FN FAL rifle

Map pocket

53

Airborne Forces

According to a Soviet "Dictionary of Basic Military Terms," an Airborne Asasult (*Vozdushnyy Desant*) comprises "Troops airlifted to the enemy rear to conduct combat activities there. According to its scale, an airborne assault may be tactical, operational or strategic. The assault may be effected either by parachute or from landed aircraft, or by a combination of both."

The first parachute unit in the world was a group of 12 Soviet soldiers who made their first appearance as a unit on August 2, 1930. Since then the Soviet Army has led the world in the development of parachute operations, and its parachute force has almost invariably been the largest in the world, as it is today. The Airborne Force is the elite of the Soviet Army, and all eight parachute divisions are stationed within the USSR in peace, thus constituting, in effect, the High Command's strategic reserve. They are considered to be politically very reliable and have always been the first elements in foreign deployments, eg, Czechoslovakia (1968), Afghanistan (1979). A clear effort is made to promote an elitist spirit, with distinctive uniforms and insignia, special weapons, and a hard, exciting training programme.

This is a most important element of the Soviet armed forces; indeed, there are suggestions that the Airborne Force could be designated a sixth independent Armed Service (alongside the Army, Navy, Air Force, National Air Defence Force, and the Strategic Rocket Forces). ▶

Right: A mass drop of Soviet paratroops. The Soviet Army was the great pioneer of airborne operations and today has the largest parachute force in the world with no less than 8 divisions at full strength.

Below: Soviet paratrooper in his jumping gear. The D-1 parachute on his back is limited to a minimum height of 492ft (150m) and a speed of 189 knots.

Right: Soviet paratroopers man a twin 23mm ZU-23 anti-aircraft weapon. There are 6 weapons per battery and one battery in each parachute regiment.

▶ Organisation

The Airborne Force is an arm of service of the Army, but is independent of the Army chain-of-command and is directly controlled by a general at the Ministry of Defence. The divisions of the Airborne Force are all maintained at Category One in peacetime, ie, they are fully manned and equipped, and have the first choice of conscript intakes. There are eight airborne divisions, one of which is responsible for training at the airborne forces depot at Tula-Ryazan.

The divisions are concentrated in Military Districts at the Western end of the USSR:

Military District	Divisions
Leningrad	1
Baltic	2
Byellorussia	1
Moscow	1
Odessa	1
Trans-Caucasus	1
Turkestan	1

There is also an independent parachute regiment at Neurippen in East Germany. These airborne divisions have a peacetime strength of some 7,200 men and are fully motorised, with some 1,500 vehicles each. The Soviets regularly practice parachute drops on a divisional scale.

Known formations are 103rd Guards Airborne Division which took Prague airport in 1968, and 105th Guards Airborne Division which took Kabul airport in December 1979 (together with elements from 103rd and 104th Guards Airborne Divisions).

Below: BMD airborne combat vehicle on parade. There are 330 in each airborne division. Infantry versions are armed with a 73mm gun, Sagger ATGW and a coaxial 7.62mm machine-gun.

▶

Above: The BMD is designed to be dropped by parachute and provides mobile firepower for Soviet parachute units. It is a well-designed and very capable fighting vehicle.

Below: Soviet paratroops and aircrew pose for a formal camera shot in front of an Ilyushin Il-76 ("Candid") aircraft. Note the blue berets and reserve parachutes worn on the chest.

57

▶ Airlift for the airborne force is provided by the Military Transport Aviation—Voyenno-Transportnaya Aviatsiya (VTA)—which is operationally subordinate to the Soviet General Staff. The VTA has a fleet of some 1,700 aircraft, including Ilyushin Il-76 (Candid), Antonov An-12 (Cub) and Antonov An-22 (Cock), all of which can be used in the parachute role. Some 200 An-12 sorties are needed to drop one airborne regiment, but this is well within Soviet capabilities, and on Exercise Dvina in 1970 a complete division was airdropped in just 22 minutes—8,000 men and 160 combat vehicles—having been flown over 620 miles (1,000km) to the drop-zone.

Weapons and equipment

The Soviet Airborne Force is so large that it is well worthwhile developing a series of special weapons and vehicles for it. Basic weapon is the AKS-74 5.45mm automatic rifle with a folding stock. Snipers use the standard-issue SVD Dragunov 7.62mm semi-automatic rifle, which, with its telescopic sight, is accurate out to 1,093 yards (1,000m).

First seen in a Moscow parade in November 1973, the *Boyevaya Machini Desnatnya* (BMD) was developed specifically for the airborne role. Though the An-12 and An-22 can both carry the BMP, it was thought that the same capability could be built into a smaller and lighter vehicle which could be dropped by parachute. The BMD had a crew of three and carries six paratroopers in open seats in the rear. It has a turret mounting a 73mm smooth-bore gun and a Sagger ATGW launcher, together with a 7.62mm PKT coaxial MG. It is also amphibious with water-jet propulsion. ▶

Right: Soviet paratroops deploy from their BMD. Note the leather helmets, one-piece suits and 7.62mm AKM assault rifles. A total of 7 men can be carried, including driver and commander.

Below: ASU-85 air-portable self-propelled anti-tank guns moving off from their Antonov An-12s. The excellent ASU-85 was first seen in 1962 and there is a battalion of 32 with each airborne division. Weapons are one 85mm anti-tank gun, one 7.62mm MG and one 12.7mm AAMG.

Above: A stick of Soviet paratroops during a winter exercise. These elite men are well-trained and enthusiastic, but suffer from the problems of a conscript army.

Above right: Paratrooper (note badge on right sleeve) carrying 5.45mm AKS-74 assault rifle. The working parts of the rifle can be seen, especially the muzzle brake and leaf backsight.

▶ Another formidable vehicle is the *Aviadesantnaya Samakhodnaia Ustanovka* (Airborne Self-Propelled Vehicle), ASU-85, first seen in 1962 and in widespread use with Soviet and other Warsaw Pact airborne units ever since. The 85mm gun has a 12 degree traverse and fires four rounds per minute. The fighting-compartment is NBC-proofed and a variety of night-fighting aids are fitted. The vehicle can be dropped by parachute, but is not amphibious.

Uniforms

The red beret is the almost universal badge of the paratrooper—except in the Soviet Army, where the colour of the beret is light blue, as are the shoulder-boards and collar tabs. There is a special paratrooper's cloth sleeve badge worn on both parade and field uniforms. All parachute divisions are "Guards" units and thus all men wear both the enamelled Guards badge and the enamelled parachute qualification badge.

Right: A political officer explains the latest issue of Pravda to an apparently happy group of paratroopers. Note the blue beret and shoulder boards and striped shirts.

Normal combat gear is a camouflaged coverall, although heavy lined jackets and trousers are worn in cold weather. A simple khaki cloth helmet is worn while jumping and on the ground, although the blue beret is also frequently worn on exercises; steel helmets do not seem to be used at all. The parachutists' badge is a stylised parachute with an aircraft each side; this is worn on the collar tabs, and is also used on all airborne forces' vehicles.

The main parachute is the D-1 model, which is limited to a maximum aircraft speed of 189 knots and a minimum height of 492 feet (150m). Static line deployment is used, although a ripcord is also fitted. A reserve parachute is carried on the chest.

Naval Infantry

The first Russian marines were raised by Peter the Great on November 16, 1705, and fought in many actions until they were disbanded following Napoleon's exile to St. Helena in 1815. Temporary marine units were raised during the Crimean War (1853-56), the Russo-Japanese War (1904-05) and the Civil War (1917-22). A permanent body was not re-established until October 18, 1941, since when, apart from a low period between 1946 and 1964, the naval infantry has become an accepted and integral part of the Soviet armed forces, and a growing threat to the West and the Third World.

Described in Russian as "morskaya pekhota" (literally: "navy infantry"), there are now some 17,500 officers and men in the force, organised into one 8,000 strong brigade based near Vladivostok with the Pacific Fleet, and one regiment each with the Northern, Baltic and Black Sea Fleets. The Soviet Naval Infantry is graded as a "guards" unit, and great emphasis is placed on the elite status this confers, to which the special uniform and accoutrements add. Like many elite forces the

Soviet Naval Infantry has its own battlecry: "Polundra", meaning "Watch out below".

Organisation

Naval Infantry regiments comprise three motor-rifle battalions (BTR-60PB APCs), a tank battalion (PT-76) an air-defence battalion (ZSU-23-4 and M8 Gecko), a multiple rocket-launcher company, and supporting engineer, signals and logistics units. The basic amphibious assault unit is the battalion group, and a likely composition was described in a recent Soviet journal: "A motorised infantry battalion detailed to operate as advanced detachment was reinforced with an artillery battery, an ATGM battery, AA, frogman and engineer platoons. It also included reconnaissance and obstacle-clearing parties, road-building teams, com- ▶

Right: Naval Infantry officer storming ashore. He carries a folding-stock 7.62mm AKMS assault rifle.

Below: Soviet Naval Infantry PT-76 Model 2 being unloaded from an Aist class air-cushion vehicle on a training exercise.

7.62mm AKMS assault rifle

Black steel helmet with red star and anchor badge

Shoulder boards with rank insignia

Map case (only officers are allowed maps)

Black combat uniform

63

▶ munications facilities, transport vehicles, and landing craft to perform transportation missions. The advanced detachment was to be supported by aviation, tactical airborne troops, support ships and minesweepers."

Selection and training

While some members of the Soviet Naval Infantry may be volunteers, most are conscripts, although, as befits its elite status, it is allocated high quality men. Units and individuals are highly trained in amphibious operations and land warfare, and, like all marines, must also know something about life on board ship as well. A very high standard of physical training is set, with particular emphasis on close-combat, especially unarmed self-defence.

Weapons and equipment

In the platoon the officer, NCOs and most marines are armed with

Below: Soviet Naval Infantry undergo very rigorous training and are expected to be equally at home on the land and at sea.

the AKM assault rifle, while the APC driver has the AKMS folding-stock version. Each squad also has an RPK machine-gun and an RPG7V anti-tank rocket launcher. Sniper teams are armed with the very effective SVD 7·62mm Dragunov sniper rifle.

Standard APC is the BTR-60PB, a well proven, 8-wheeled amphibious vehicle. This may well be replaced in the future by the new BTR-70, which is basically a product-improved BTR-60PB. The BMP tracked APC is also known to be in service with the Soviet Naval Infantry. Standard amphibious tank is the PT-76; the current version is the PT-76 Model 2 which has minor modifications to the main gun, but it would seem that a replacement for this very old vehicle must be due soon. The main advantage of the BTR-60PB and the PT-76 is that they enable the leading elements of an assault landing to enter the water off the beach and swim ashore, which may be an invaluable ability in certain situations. T-54/55 main battle tanks serve with the Soviet Naval Infantry; they are not amphi-

64

bious and would land in the second wave from landing-craft direct over the beaches.

The BM-21 rocket launcher is used for artillery support. The ZSU-23-4 AA gun and SA-8 Gecko are both used for air defence; both vehicles are amphibious. Surprisingly, little emphasis seems to have ▶

Above: Polnocny class LSTs of the Soviet Navy unloading BTR 60PB APCs and a PT-76 reconnaissance tank.

Below: Black uniform, striped T-shirt and anchor device on helmet and sleeve clearly identify the Soviet Naval Infantry.

Above: Beachmaster (with flags) controlling a landing. In an amphibious landing the SNI always leave their vehicles at the waters-edge, rendering them very vulnerable.

▶ been put on helicopters until relatively recently, although some Mil Mi-8 Hips are now being deployed for use in "vertical assault" type operations.

Uniform

The uniform of the Soviet Naval Infantry is a combination of army and navy items, with a few unique embellishments of their own. Combat dress is a black suit, with calf-length black leather boots. A black leather belt is also worn, with the appropriate fleet badge on the buckle. A horizontally striped blue and white tee-shirt is standard with all forms of dress. The usual range of Soviet metal award brooches is worn, with all officers and men wearing the "Guards" badge. A round cloth badge with an embroidered anchor is worn on the left sleeve just above the elbow.

Various items of headgear are worn. In assault operations a black steel helmet is worn with a large five-pointed red star on the front, and a stencilled anchor inside a broken anchor on the left. On other occasions a soft black beret is worn with a small anchor badge above the left ear; the main badge is a large enamelled naval badge for officers and a small red star for NCOs and marines.

Amphibious shipping

The Soviet Naval Infantry would be of limited value without special-role shipping, and a whole range of purpose-built craft has been developed. Largest of these is the Ivan Rogov class of 14,000-ton Landing Platform Dock (LPD), of which two are now in service. Capable of carrying a complete battalion group with all its vehicles and supporting arms, the Rogov is a significant addition to the Soviet global capability. Next are some 14 Ropucha class and 16 Alligator class Landing Ship Tanks (LST), both of some 4,500 tons displacement, and there is an ever-increasing number of smaller vessels. Particular investment has been made in the area of air-cushion vehicles (ACV) with the Aist class unique in the world's amphibious forces.

Although not specifically designed for the purpose it is clear that carriers of the Kiev and Moskva class could also be used to transport naval infantry units, and that their flight-decks would be particularly valuable for heli-borne landings.

Below: A riverine operation by SNI. This force is regarded as one of the Soviet elites and has "guards" status, which is not granted lightly. Their training programme is arduous and keeps them at a high pitch, vital for troops which could be used at short notice anywhere in the world. They have provided a new and very significant dimension to Soviet military power.

Spetsnaz

Spetsnaz units are an outcome of the Soviet experiences in World War II, and appear to have started in the early 1950s, although it is only very recently that their existence has become public knowledge in the West. Spetsnaz are the special forces of the GRU, the Soviet Military Intelligence organisation; they are also known as "diversionary troops" and their units as "diversionary brigades". Spetsnaz war tasks are believed to include murder of enemy political and military leaders; attacks on enemy nuclear bases and command centres; and general attacks on military and civil targets (eg, power supplies) intended to create panic and disruption. In peace Spetsnaz forces number some 27,000 to 30,000, making them by far the largest special forces group in the world, and serve both the Soviet Army and Navy.

Organisation

It is estimated that in war the Soviets will have one independent Spetsnaz company per Army (total 41), one Spetsnaz brigade per Front (total 16), one Spetsnaz brigade per Fleet (total 4), one Spetsnaz regiment per Commander-in-Chief of Central Direction (equivalent to a Western "theatre of operations") (total 3), plus one Spetsnaz intelligence unit per Front and Fleet (total 20). An independent Spetsnaz company consists of 9 officers, 11 warrant officers and 95 men, a much higher proportion of officers and warrant officers than in ordinary "line" units. These normally operate in up to 15 separate groups, but can come together into fewer groups (or even one unit) for specific actions.

A Spetsnaz brigade has an HQ, an anti-VIP company (70 to 80 strong), 3 or 4 battalions, a signal company and supporting units. The brigade, 1,000 to 1,300 strong, can split up into some 135 groups. The anti-VIP company is trained to find, identify and kill enemy political and military leaders, and is composed exclusively of regular troops (ie, there are no conscripts in this sub-unit).

The naval Spetsnaz brigade has an anti-VIP company, a group of midget submarines, 2 or 3 battalions of combat swimmers, a parachute battalion and supporting units. The Spetsnaz regiments are some 700 to 800 strong, are split into 6 or 7 "sabotage" companies, and are manned exclusively by professional athletes; indeed, it has even been suggested that the bulk of the modern Soviet Olympic teams have come from these units. ▶

Right: Spetsnaz soldier with SA-7 Grail missile launcher. His war tasks would take him deep into NATO rear areas.

Below: One of the essentials for Spetsnaz soldiers is a very high standard of physical fitness, even up to Olympic standard if possible.

Protective goggles
always used with SA-7

Camouflaged
hood

SA-7 Grail
shoulder-
launched anti-
aircraft
missile

Camouflage
combat
uniform

RGD-5 anti-
personnel hand
grenade

Russian boots

69

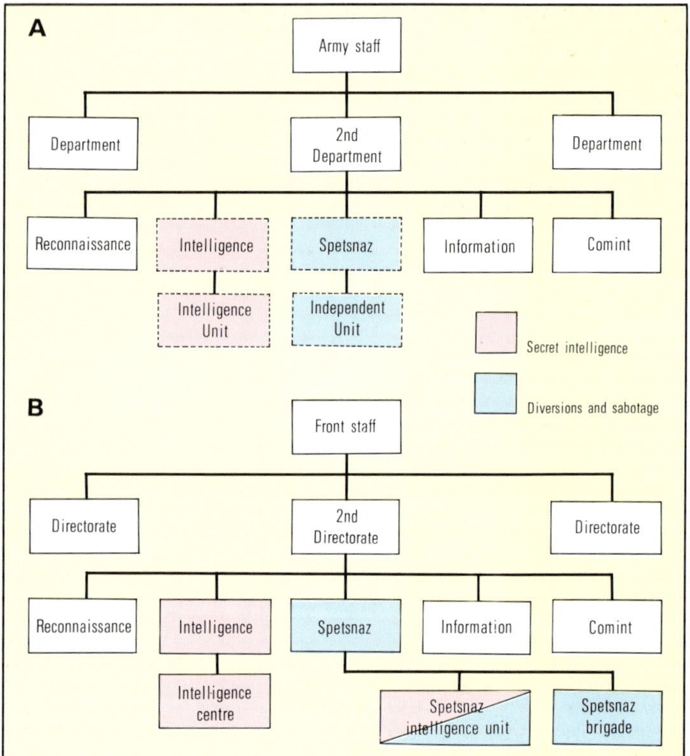

A

- Army staff
  - Department
  - 2nd Department
    - Reconnaissance
    - Intelligence
      - Intelligence Unit
    - Spetsnaz
      - Independent Unit
    - Information
    - Comint
  - Department

Secret intelligence

Diversions and sabotage

B

- Front staff
  - Directorate
  - 2nd Directorate
    - Reconnaissance
    - Intelligence
      - Intelligence centre
    - Spetsnaz
      - Spetsnaz intelligence unit
      - Spetsnaz brigade
    - Information
    - Comint
  - Directorate

C

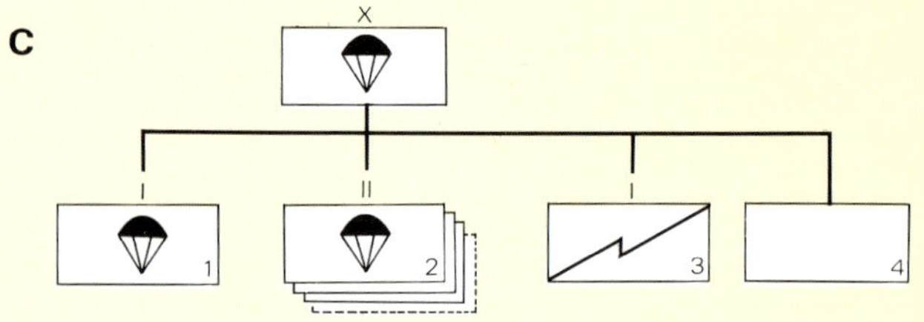

1 — HQ company (anti-VIP) 2 — Parachute battalions 3 — Signals company 4 — Supporting units

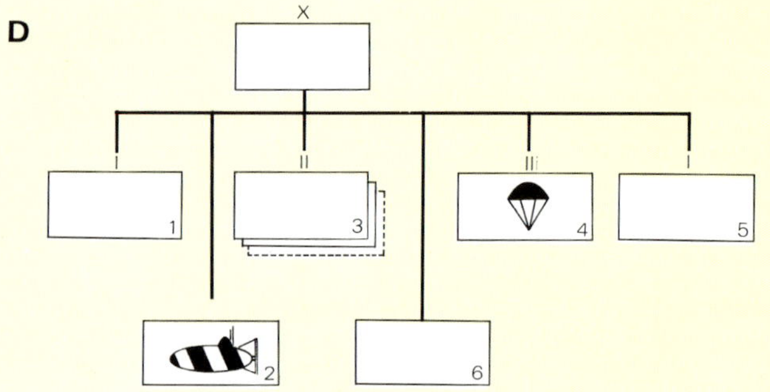

D

1 — HQ company (anti-VIP) 2 — Midget submarine group 3 — Combat swimmer battalions 4 — Parachute battalion
5 — Signals company 6 — Supporting units

Information derived from a Viktor Suvorov article in International Defense Review

Selection and training

For conscript soldiers, who make up the bulk of Spetsnaz units in peace, the selection process starts well before they join the Army, through the aegis of the DOSAAF system of preliminary military training and political assessment. On call-up the conscripts assessed to have Spetsnaz potential undergo a short and very intensive course, and those who show up best are sent on to another and much tougher training battalion to become sergeants. Many more sergeants are trained than there are vacancies for (those who are not selected serve as private soldiers in Spetsnaz units), thus giving an inbuilt reserve of qualified leaders.

Specialist courses are run in languages, foreign countries, demolitions, special communications, and so on.

Officers and warrant officers receive a 50 per cent pay enhancement, as well as parachute jumping pay. Peacetime training is intense and there is a regular series of very arduous exercises, with considerable efforts being made to ensure that these are as realistic as possible. Once a year most Spetsnaz units are assembled in the USSR for a period of collective training.

Weapons and equipment

On operations every Spetsnaz soldier would carry a 5.45mm AKS-74 rifle with some 3 to 400 rounds of ammunition, a P6 silenced pistol (or the new 5.45mm PRI automatic pistol), combat knife and six hand-grenades. Each soldier carries rations and medical kit, and each group has an R-350M radio set (with encryption and burst-transmission). The group may also carry an SA-7 SAM launcher, mines, explosives, light grenade-launchers and other equipment appropriate to their particular mission. For those infiltrated into hostile countries prior to the outbreak of war such equipment would be smuggled in to in-place agents ready for issue when the time came. The groups could be expected to avail themselves of cars, lorries, motor-cycles, etc, either provided by agents, or stolen during operations.

Uniform

In order to preserve their "cover" Spetsnaz units have no special uniform or badges. In the USSR they wear the same uniform as the airborne forces and air assault ▶

Left: Spetsnaz control organisation at Army (A) and Front/Fleet (B) levels. Peacetime organisation is into army brigades (C) and naval brigades (D). In war Spetsnaz would fight in small groups coming together into larger groups for specific operations.

Below: Soviet paratroops (almost certainly Spetsnaz) on a typical Soviet army assault course. The rifle is the new 5.45mm AKS-74 with folding butt and 30-round plastic magazine.

▶ troops, although (unlike the airborne forces) Spetsnaz and air assault troops do not wear the special "Guards unit" badge. In non-Soviet Warsaw Pact countries Spetsnaz troops wear the uniform of the communications troops whose barracks they share. In Spetsnaz naval brigades the special troops wear naval infantry uniforms, except for the midget submarine crews who wear normal submariners' gear. Several sources state that in a general war Spetsnaz troops would wear NATO uniforms or civilian clothes wherever the need arose.

Tactics

Spetsnaz tactical troops will be dropped by parachute deep into enemy territory at the very start of hostilities: Front brigades 310 to 620 miles (500 to 1,000km) and Army companies 62 to 310 miles (100 to 500km). This will be a massive and coordinated operation, and could well use aircraft in Aeroflot (as opposed to military) markings. Top priority targets will

Below: Spetsnaz troops would be used to attack NATO forces and installations in wartime. Their training grounds (such as that depicted) include accurate mock-ups of NATO equipments, especially those with a nuclear role, such as GLCM.

be nuclear-delivery means, such as missile sites, cruise-missile launchers, etc, as well as causing maximum confusion as the enemy attempts to deploy for war.

Spetsnaz troops with strategic tasks may well be infiltrated into target countries prior to hostilities, disguised as tourists, sports teams, cultural groups, businessmen, or members of diplomatic missions. Entry to the target country may well be by way of a third country. These groups will obviously wear civilian clothes, and will use in-place sleeper agents wherever possible as guides and sources of information, shelter and transportation. Naval Spetsnaz units will infiltrate mainly by sea, using submarines to approach close to their targets and then reaching shore by midget submarines, inflatables or by swimming. Their primary targets will be naval nuclear bases, such as the Britain's Royal Navy base at Faslane, Scotland, and the French base at Toulon, Southern France.

A Spetsnaz battalion is said to have been the first Soviet unit into Czechoslovakia during the "uprising" in 1968, having had the task of seizing Prague airport, thus enabling the following 103rd Guards Airborne Division to land unhindered. Spetsnaz troops have also operated in Afghanistan, and are almost certainly still there.

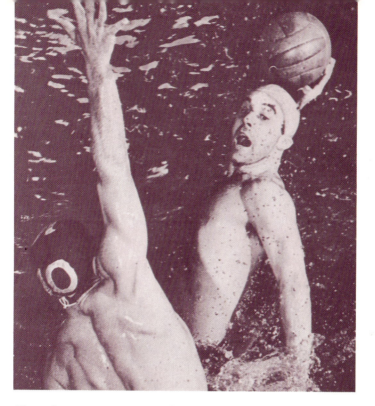

Above: Spetsnaz troops must, of course, be extremely fit and the USSR also fields excellent sports teams in world events. In fact, they combine the two requirements and there are many cases of athletes later being identified as members of covert units.

Below: India class submarine is the "mother-ship" for tracked mini-subs operated by naval Spetsnaz units. Such mini-subs have been used in Swedish waters in 1983 and tracks were found on the sea-bed, evidence of Soviet preparation for war.

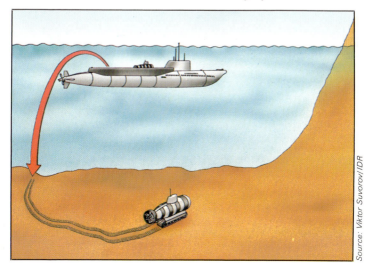

Long Range Amphibious Reconnaissance Commandos

When Chiang Kai-shek and the last of the Nationalist Chinese forces were compelled to leave mainland China on December 7, 1949, they swore that one day they would return. Today, 35 years later, that remains their stated aim despite the immense power of the Communist mainland and virtual abandonment by the USA. So great is this determination that the government even issues two annual budgets: one "provincial" budget for Taiwan, and a second "national" budget for the mainland.

The Army is very efficient and well-trained, and is currently some 330,000 strong. Their deployment is split between the main island of Taiwan, some 100 miles (160km) offshore, and the two inshore islands of Quemoy and Matsu, both of which are within artillery range of the mainland. The Quemoy garrison is some 60,000 strong and that of Matsu some 20,000. There have been several crises over this situation, particularly in 1954, 1955 and 1957 but, although there have been no overwhelming threats of late, the potential for trouble remains. The government on Taiwan maintains very large armed forces, which are very efficient and highly trained, but are also a substantial drain on the economy.

Included in Taiwan's army are four special forces groups, which include the Long-Range Amphibious Reconnaissance Commandos, and para-frogmen. There are also two brigades of paratroopers. The Recce Commandos are very highly trained and are known to have been active on the mainland in the maritime provinces for many years.

There is a growing relationship, including between special forces, between the four isolated countries of Israel, South Africa, Singapore and Taiwan. Advisers are exchanged, weapons bought and sold, and "know-how" passed from one to another.

Weapons and equipment

Standard rifle of the Taiwan Army is the M16A1, of which some 5,000 have been supplied direct from the USA. The Combined Services Arsenal at Kaohsuing has, however, produced a new rifle—designated the 5.56mm Type 65—which is now in service with Taiwan special forces, including the Long-Range Amphibious Reconnaissance Commandos. This bears some similarities to the M16A1, although it also has features taken from the AR-18 design.

The standard sub-machine gun is the 0.45 Type 36, a locally produced version of the US M3A1. Standard light machine-gun is the US M60 7.62mm, made under licence in Taiwan. Obtaining weapons is becoming a major problem as the PRC imposes pressure on former suppliers.

Uniform

Up till now the uniform of the Taiwanese forces has been almost totally American in design and appearance, although this influence may diminish as the USA seeks closer ties with the People's Republic and distances itself more and more from its former allies on Taiwan.

Right: Soldier of Taiwan's elite Long-Range Recce Commandos demonstrates his martial arts prowess. Western forces are at last starting to appreciate the value of such skills and are teaching them to their special forces. Not only do such martial arts train men in unarmed combat techniques, but they also improve physical fitness and mental discipline. Taiwan's commandos have much combat experience and have been active on the offshore islands, and probably on the mainland as well, since the Kuomintang forces were expelled from the mainland in December 1949.

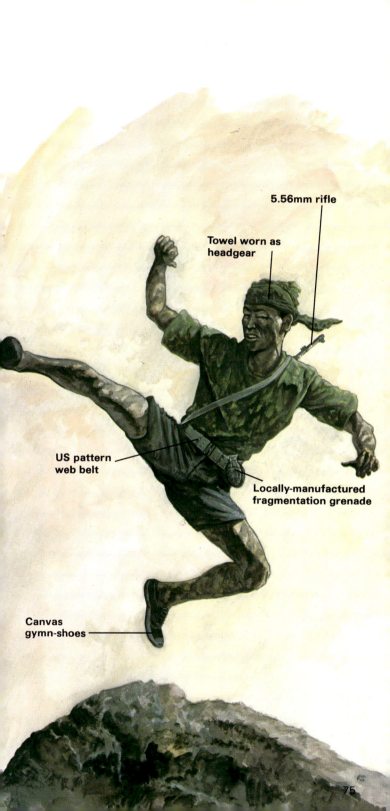

5.56mm rifle

Towel worn as
headgear

US pattern
web belt

Locally-manufactured
fragmentation grenade

Canvas
gymn-shoes

75

Army Special Forces

Thailand has long had both external and internal defence problems. The Communist insurgents in Malaysia have used southern Thailand as a sanctuary for many years, and they have had repeated clashes with the Thai military forces. There are also tensions on the border with Burma, but the biggest problems are on the eastern border with Kampuchea, where the Royal Thai Army finds itself face-to-face with the Vietnamese Army, the most experienced land force in Asia.

The Royal Thai Army had an airborne Ranger battalion for some years and in 1963 this was reorganised and redesignated 1st Special Forces Group (Airborne); since then 2nd, 3rd and 4th Special Forces Groups have been raised, and were recently redesignated regiments. Their tasks include unconventional warfare behind the enemy lines, psychological operations, civic actions and, above all, counter-insurgency. One of the principal activities in the counter-insurgency field is the organisation, training and equipping of village defence units to look after village defence and also to provide support for army (and especially, of course, Special Forces) operations in their areas.

Organisation

In July 1982 the four Special Forces regiments were consolidated into a new formation: 1st Special Forces Division. This is commanded by Major-General Wimol Wongwanich and the HQ is at Fort Narai in Lophuri province. This division comprises the four Special Forces regiments, together with a psychological operations (psyops) bat-

Above: After a ha-lo jump a Thai special forces trooper secures his parachute. Note the black combat uniform and helmet.

talion, long-range reconnaissance patrol (LRRP) company and the Special Warfare Centre.

Selection and training

Volunteers for the Special Forces must first complete both parachute and Ranger schools before admission to the Special Forces regiments where they undergo further training. There is also a survival centre, where the many specialised skills of jungle survival are taught.

Great attention is paid to physical fitness, especially to a form of martial arts based upon traditional Thai boxing, a highly effective activity which involves the use not

Left: Thai Special Forces soldier in the jungle which covers a large part of his country. Tough and determined fighters, the Thai soldiers have been fighting Communist guerrillas since the 1950s and now face the Vietnamese.

Above: Martial art is based on Thai boxing, a traditional sport, requiring great fitness as well as suppleness and courage.

only of the hands, but of feet as well. There is also emphasis on parachute training.

Weapons and equipment

The Thai Special Forces use US equipment and weapons; the basic weapon, for example, is the M16 rifle. Like most Special Forces they also train on foreign weapons likely to be used by any potential enemies.

Uniform

The main symbol of the Special Forces is a red beret with a gold woven national army capbadge. Working uniform is a two-piece camouflage suit, with low-visibility black embroidered rank and qualification badges. The same uniform is worn on operations, but with a camouflaged "jungle hat". A special combat uniform is also sometimes used, comprising a black suit and black boots, topped with a black knitted balaclava helmet; an outfit obviously modelled on that used by the British SAS.

Gurkhas

The bonds which link the legendary Gurkhas from the hills of Nepal with the British Army are slightly difficult to understand, but their strength is self-evident. The British in India fought two short wars against the Gurkhas in 1813 and 1816, which resulted in a very hard-won British victory and considerable mutual respect for each other's martial qualities. As a result three battalions of Gurkhas were immediately raised (1815) and Gurkhas have served the British Crown ever since.

For well over a century the Gurkhas were part of the British Indian Army, but when the British left India in 1947 the Gurkha units were split between the new Indian Army (where some 80,000 still serve) and the British Army. The British Gurkhas moved to Malaya where these redoubtable mountain warriors became highly respected jungle fighters, playing a significant role in the defeat of the Malayan Communists. These skills stood them in good stead when they took part in the "confrontation" campaign in Borneo against the Indonesians. Following the end of that little war in 1967, and with the departure of the British from Malaya, the Gurkhas moved their base to Hong Kong, where they have been ever since.

The Gurkhas' most recent campaign was in 1982 when 1st Battalion, 7th Duke of Edinburgh's Own Gurkha Rifles (1/7GR) went to the Falkland Islands as part of 5 Infantry Brigade. They landed in San Carlos Bay and spent their first week mounting patrols to round up Argentine stragglers. On June 8 they went to Bluff Cove and then on to join in the final attacks on the Argentine positions around Port Stanley. The Argentine soldiers were quite literally terrified of the Gurkhas, who they accused of being "high" on drugs and of mercilessly killing any prisoners. Nothing could be further from the truth; the Gurkhas have always been known to fight hard, but then to be generous in victory. But it would be idle to deny that the Gurkhas had a very poor opinion of the Argentine soldiers who fled at the first sign that they were facing the famed Gurkha Rifles.

Organisation

The original three battalions expanded and changed titles over the years, but basically there have been 10 regiments (of varying numbers of battalions) for most of the Gurkhas' history. In 1947 when the British left India the 1st, 4th, 5th, 8th and 9th Gurkha Rifles went to the Indian Army, and the balance—2nd, 6th, 7th and 10th Gurkha Rifles—to the British Army. Still serving in the British Army are: 2nd King Edward VII's Own Goorkhas (The Sirmoor Rifles), two battalions; 6th Queen Elizabeth's Own Gurkha Rifles; 7th Duke of Edinburgh's Own Gurkha Rifles, (two battalions); 10th Princess Mary's Own Gurkha Rifles.

Individual battalions are on the standard British Army organisation, with some very minor amendments to comply with regimental custom. Following their move to the British Army the Gurkhas expanded their activities to include engineers, signals and transportation. At times there have also been Gurkha artillery, parachute troops and military police, but these have all been disbanded.

The infantry battalions have very few British officers, the great majority being Queen's Gurkha Officers who have worked their way up through the ranks to Warrant Officer before being commissioned. The most senior is the Gurkha Major, a figure of immense prestige, who is the Commanding Officer's adviser on all Gurkha matters.

The principal current formation is the Gurkha Field Force (equivalent to a brigade) which is located at Sek Kong Camp in the New Territories in Hong Kong. This comprises four Gurkha battalions, of which one is detached to Brunei where it serves (and is paid for by) the Sultan. There is one battalion in ▶

British Army '58 pattern webbing equipment

British Army jungle hat with battalion recognition band

Olive-green jungle uniform

Ration pouch

US M16A1 5.56mm rifle

Gurkha kukri in green canvas combat scabbard

Jungle boots

Above: This Gurkha rifleman comes from the hills of Nepal, but has become one of the finest jungle fighters in the world. His rifle is the US M16A1, but he also carries his famed kukri knife.

▶ England, stationed near Aldershot, and another in a training role in Hong Kong.

Selection and training

Gurkhas are recruited from the hill tribesmen in the Himalayan kingdom of Nepal. There are always far more volunteers than there are vacancies so the British recruiting officers can afford to very selective. Enlisting at 17½ years of age, Gurkhas serve for a minimum of five years, and the best continue for up to 32 years, leaving at age

Below: A company commander (major) and his radio operator of the 6th Gurkha Rifles (6GR) leading a patrol in dense jungle. Fighting for Britain for some 170 years, the Gurkhas' latest battlefield was the Falklands.

50. Recruit intakes arrive in Hong Kong in January of every year and train for nine months.

Uniform and weapons

Gurkhas wear their own variations of British Army uniform. Combat kit is standard camouflage pattern smock and trousers, with green canvas webbing, except, of course, for the addition of the famous kukri. Parade uniform is rifle-green in temperate climates and white in the tropics, with black, patent-leather waist belts for soldiers and cross-belts for officers. Buttons and badges are black. Soldiers wear a black pill-box hat on parade or the Gurkha slouch-hat, and a green beret in other forms of dress.

The kukri is the subject of many myths. The knives come in various sizes, but the dog-legged shape is

constant. The rear edge is thick and blunt, making the knife quite heavy, but the cutting-edge is razor sharp.

The kukri is in no way a throwing knife, but it is quite excellent for hand-to-hand fighting and is the Gurkhas' preferred close-combat weapon. It is therefore always carried in war and there are many stories of its use against Germans, Japanese and Malayan Communists, to mention but a few of the Gurkhas' more recent enemies. They were also, no doubt, keen to test them on Argentinians but were frustrated by the latter's rapid departure.

The future

With the prospect of the British departure from Hong Kong in 1997 the future of the British Gurkhas is once more in doubt. One or two battalions might be sustained in the United Kingdom, but this would be very expensive. Nevertheless it would be a very sad day were the ties between these legendary soldiers and the British Crown they have served so well to be severed.

Above: A British officer with his riflemen of the 10th Gurkha Rifles. The relationship between men and their officers is very close and is based upon mutual trust and respect—and tradition.

Nowhere is the depth of this unique relationship more clearly described than in (of all places) the introduction to a Nepali language dictionary compiled by Sir Ralph Turner some sixty years ago: "As I write these last words, my thoughts return to you who were my comrades, the stubborn and indomitable peasants of Nepal. Once more I hear the laughter with which you greeted every hardship. Once more I see you in your bivouacs or about your fires, on forced march or in the trenches, now shivering with wet and cold, now scorched by a pitiless and burning sun. Uncomplaining, you endure hunger and thirst and wounds, and at last your unwavering lines disappear into the smoke and wrath of battle. Bravest of the brave, most generous of the generous, never had a country more faithful friends than you."

Parachute Regiment

The very name of the Parachute Regiment (the "paras") has come to signify both a type of soldiering and a certain "style"—dramatic, forceful and with panache. Paratroops would, it seems, always need to be fighting against heavy odds and either succeed brilliantly or suffer glorious defeats: the one performance that is never allowed is an indifferent one.

Inevitably it was Winston Churchill who demanded that a slightly reluctant War Office should establish a corps of parachutists on the German model and after a somewhat hesitant start the first unit was formed in late 1940. A trial operation against an aqueduct in Italy in February 1941 ended up with little damage to the objective and all the men captured. However, lessons were learned and progress was made.

The 6th Airborne Division landed on the Allied left flank on D-Day June 6, 1944, and successfully accomplished all its tasks, although it suffered when left in the line for some two months as a conventional infantry unit. That episode over, the paras were withdrawn to England and their next employment was at Arnhem where 1st Airborne Division performed with the most exemplary courage, but were in the end overcome, their reputation made for all time. 6th Airborne Division then took part in the Rhine crossings, which went very well.

When World War II ended the paratroops found themselves involved in two activities which have kept them very busy up to the present day. The first has been to fight their country's many small wars in numerous campaigns on virtually every continent. These conflicts have taken the paras to Malaya, Borneo, Palestine, Suez, Aden, Cyprus, Kuwait, North Borneo and Northern Ireland and the Falkland Islands. Their second major post-war campaign has been one of stubborn resistance to the War Office and the Ministry of Defence in its efforts to dispose of the Parachute Regiment altogether.

Right: Corporal of The Parachute Regiment on patrol in Northern Ireland. He is wearing a "flak" vest and carrying a 7.62mm L1A1 Self-Loading Rifle (SLR).

Below: Parachute Regiment anti-tank team wearing the famous, but now outmoded, paratroops helmets and "Dennison" camouflage smocks.

There was a major reduction in parachute troops in the immediate post-war years, and again in the 1960s and 1970s. 16th Parachute Brigade existed in Aldershot from 1949 to 1977 when it was redesignated 6 Field Force in one of the British Army's endless series of reorganisations and only one battalion of the Parachute Regiment was left in the parachute role, with the two other battalions serving elsewhere in the "straight" infantry role. On 1 January 1982 6th Field Force became 5 Infantry Brigade and included among its units 2nd and 3rd Battalions The Parachute Regiment.

When the South Atlantic War blew up suddenly in 1982 these two battalions were hived off to 3 Commando Brigade and sent south with the Marines. In the Falklands these two units performed very well, and at Goose Green 550 men of 2 Para took on 1,400 Argentines and defeated them utterly, even though their commanding officer,

Lt. Col. "H" Jones, died in the battle. In the finest para tradition he died at the head of his men, personally leading an attack against a machine-gun position that was holding up the entire attack. He was posthumously awarded the Victoria Cross.

The paras' methods are nothing if not direct and this has, on several occasions, made them controversial. They have always been among the more successful units in Northern Ireland and thus naturally a target for hostile propaganda. This reached a nadir on January 30, 1972, in the so-called "Bloody Sunday" episode when a crowd of civilians attacked the paras and in the ensuing action some 13 civilians were killed. There was an enormous outcry, but despite this the battalions of the Parachute Regiment have continued to return to Northern Ireland.

In December 1982 the British Secretary of State for Defence, Michael Heseltine, went to Alder- ▶

▶ shot to announce in person that 5 Infantry Brigade was to be redesignated 5 Airborne Brigade forthwith, so it would appear that the existence of the British Parachute Regiment is secure for a few more years.

Organisation

There are currently three battalions of the Parachute Regiment in the British regular army (1, 2 and 3 Para), and a further three battalions in the Territorial Army (4, 10 and 15 Para). Two of the three regular battalions are part of 5 Airborne Brigade. This brigade does not, however, currently have parachute-trained and equipped supporting units (artillery, engineers, transport, etc) necessary for a full airborne deployment, but this may return with time.

Selection and training

The infantry battalions of the Parachute Regiment recruit direct from civilian life. There is tough selection and training course held at the regimental depot at Aldershot.

Weapons and equipment

When there was an independent parachute force (16 Parachute Brigade) there was sufficient demand for it to be economical to produce special equipment for paratroop units. When the commitment was reduced in the past few years to just two parachute battalions in the parachute role, with virtually no back-up from parachute-trained and -equipped supporting arms and services, such special equipment virtually disappeared. Thus, UK parachute units currently use standard British Army weapons and equipment, such as the 7.62mm L1A1 rifle, 9mm L2A3 Sterling sub-machine gun and L7A1 7.62mm general-purpose machine-gun.

However, the British Army is shortly to be issued with the 5.56mm L70A1 Individual Weapon, also known as the Small Arm for the 80s (SA80), an excellent weapon using the "bull-pup" design. This rifle is neat, compact and well-balanced and has proved very popular in troop trials. It can be expected that the battalions of the Parachute Regiment will be among the earliest to receive this weapon and its light-machine gun version, the L73A1.

Uniforms

The British paratroops' red beret has been adopted around the world and has given rise to their nicknames of "The Red Devils" and "The Red Berets". (History has it that Major-General Browning and

Wireless Ridge June 13-14, 1982

The battalion attack by 2nd Battalion, The Parachute Regiment (2 Para) on Wireless Ridge, on June 13-14 during the Falklands War in 1982, is an excellent example of an action by a highly trained, fit and experienced infantry unit. This action is of particular interest because 2 Para were the only battalion in the Falklands War to carry out two battalion attacks, and thus the only one to be able to put into practice the lessons learned, in their case at such high cost at Goose Green on May 28.

On June 11, 2 Para was moved by helicopter from Fitzroy on the south coast to a lying-up position west of Mount Kent. At 2300 hours the battalion set off on foot to an assembly area on a hill to the North of Mount Kent, ready to support either 3 Para in their attack on Mount Longdon or 45 Commando Royal Marines, whose mission was to take the position known as Two Sisters. Both these attacks were successful, leaving 3 Para, 45 Commando and 42 Commando firmly established. On June 12, 2 Para moved forward some 9 miles (15km), skirting Mount Longdon on its north-western side, to an assembly area in the lee of a ▶

Right: En route to war, and in a strange environment, British paratroops man machine-guns on board a ship in the South Atlantic in 1982.

another general were arguing over the colour of a beret for the paratroops sometime in 1942 and, being unable to agree, they turned to the nearest soldier and asked for his views. "Red, sir," came the instant answer.) The red beret can be worn only by members of the Parachute Regiment (throughout their service) and by members of other Corps who are parachute-

Above: British paratrooper on a landing zone with another just landed right behind him. Full effectiveness requires constant, hard and realistic training.

qualified, but only when on service with a parachute unit. The sleeve badge of the winged Pegasus was designed by Edward Seago, a famous artist.

steep escarpment which offered some cover from the sporadic shelling by the respected Argentine artillery. The battalion, as always, dug-in; orders were received in mid-afternoon for an attack on Wireless Ridge that night, but this was later postponed to the following night.

On June 13 Skyhawk attack aircraft flew in low from the West. Intense fire from the ground prevented the attack from being pressed home, but a number of moves in preparation for the forthcoming battalion action were delayed, especially the registration of targets by the artillery and mortars. At Goose Green 2 Para had been very short of fire support, but in this battle they were to have two batteries of 105mm light guns in direct support, the mortars of both 2 and 3 Para, naval gunfire support from ships within range, as well as the battalion's own machine-gun and MILAN anti-tank missile platoons. Last, but by no means least, a troop of two Scimitar (1 x 30mm cannon) and two Scorpion (1 x 76mm gun) light tanks of The Blues and Royals were an integral part of 2 Para's battle plan.

The battalion moved out at last light (2030 hours local). As they moved to the Forming-Up Places (FUPs), where the troops shake out into battle formations, the sort of report a commanding officer dreads was received: that Intelligence had just discovered a minefield in front of A and B Companies' objective. At this stage, however, there was no alternative but to go ahead.

Right: The Battle of Wireless Ridge took place on June 13/14, 1982, during the South Atlantic War. It was a highly successful battalion attack, incorporating the lessons learned earlier in the brief land campaign. D Company (D) started by taking the Western end of the ridge, following which A Company (A) and B Company (B) took the main position. C Company (C) provided flank protection to the east. Fire support came from tanks, artillery and ships.

The artillery supporting fire started at 0015 hours on June 14 and D Company crossed the start-line at 0045 hours. D Company reached its first objective with little trouble, finding that the enemy had withdrawn, leaving a few dead in their slit trenches. While D Company reorganised, enemy 155mm airburst fire began to fall on their position, a reminder of the efficiency and quick reactions of the Argentine artillery. Meanwhile, A and B Companies began their advance, B Company through what transpired to be the minefield recently discovered by Intelligence.

Some sporadic fire came from a few trenches, but was quickly silenced, and 17 prisoners were taken and a number killed in this ▶

Right: Machine-gunners of the Parachute Regiment training on-board ship. Their weapon is the 7.62mm L7A2 (GPMG).

3 PARA

45 CDO

2 SG

42 CDO

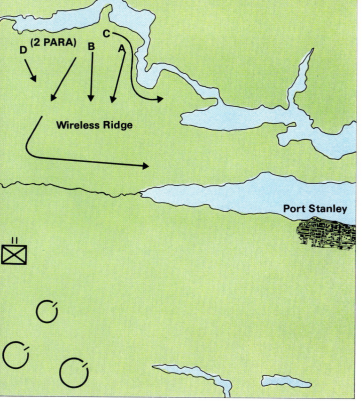

▶ phase of the battle—the remainder fled. Several radios (still switched on), telephones and a mass of cable suggested that the position had included a battalion head-quarters. Once again, as A and B Companies started to dig in, an accurate and fairly intense enemy artillery bombardment began, and in fact continued for some nine hours.

Following the success of A and B Companies, D Company crossed its second start line at the West end of the main ridge, while the light tanks and the machine-guns moved to a flank to give covering fire. The ridge itself was a long spire broken in the middle, with each section some 900 yards (300m) in length. The first feature was taken unopposed and there was then a short delay while the British artillery readjusted to its targets for the next phase. During this time the second feature was kept under heavy fire by the light tanks, the machine-guns and the MILAN missile being used in a direct-fire artillery role!

Just as the attack was about to start the commanding officer received a new piece of intelligence, that instead of one enemy company at the other end of the ridge there were two! This was hardly likely to impress the Paras who by this stage of the campaign had estab-lished a considerable moral ascend-

Above: British paratroops search captured Argentine soldiers in the 1982 South Atlantic war.

Right: Paras on the Falkland Islands manning a 7.62mm GPMG mounted on a tripod in the sustained fire role.

ency over the Argentines, but in the early minutes of this final phase of the battle D Company did receive some casualties as the enemy fought back with unexpect-ed vigour, withdrawing one bunker at a time. As the paras poured onto the position, however, the enemy suddenly broke and ran, being continuously harassed off the position by the machine-guns of the British Scorpions and Scimitars, and chased by the exhilarated paras.

As D Company began to re-organise they, too, came under artillery fire, as well as remarkably effective small arms fire from Tumbledown Mountain and Mount William to the South, which had not yet been captured by 5 Infantry Brigade. The enemy could be heard trying to regroup in the darkness below the ridge, and to the south in the area of Moody Brook. At daybreak a rather brave, but somewhat pathetic counter-attack developed from the area of Moody Brook, which seems to have been some sort of final gesture. It petered out within a few minutes under a hail of artillery, small arms and machine-gun fire.

This seems to have been the signal to many Argentines that the game was up, and shortly afterwards ever-increasing numbers of disheartened and disillusioned Argentine soldiers were observed streaming off Mount William, Tumbledown and Sapper Hill to seek an apparent (but very short-lived) refuge in Port Stanley. A and B Companies of 2 Para were now brought forward onto Wireless Ridge, and the battalion's night attack was successfully concluded. The paras had lost three dead and 11 wounded. Lack of time and opportunity precluded counting the Argentine casualties, but it has been estimated that, of an original strength of some 500, up to 100 may have been killed, 17 were captured, and the remainder fled.

The taking of Wireless Ridge illustrates the standards achieved by a crack unit. In this night battle it totally defeated a force of equal strength, well prepared and dug-in, and occupying a dominant feature. No. 2 Para had been through the traumatic experience of the Goose Green battle earlier in the campaign, but had learned the lessons well. They had also given the lie to the allegation that parachute units do not have "staying power". It is, perhaps, unfortunate that the battle of Goose Green, deservedly famous, has overshadowed this later minor classic at Wireless Ridge.

Royal Marines Special Boat Squadron

To a large extent the whole of the Royal Marines is an elite force in itself; every marine would certainly claim it so. However, the Royal Marines are basically very highly trained infantry, optimised for the amphibious role.

Within the Royal Marines there are a number of smaller and more select groups of which the best known and most highly trained is the Special Boat Squadron (SBS). This squadron has its roots in the special units raised in World War II for raiding and reconnaissance on the shores of the European mainland. The techniques evolved so painfully in war were, fortunately, preserved in peace, despite many cutbacks and amalgamations. The Amphibious School of the Royal Marines at Eastney (now at Poole in Dorset) included a "Small Raids Wing", which was later redesig-

nated the "Special Boat Company" and then, in 1977, the "Special Boat Squadron".

The SBS is the headquarters for the Special Boat Sections which are deployed under the operational command of Commando units, but can also act autonomously on special tasks. The major role of the SBS is in amphibious operations, especially on reconnaissance, sabotage and demolitions. They are also believed to have particular responsibilities in the security of Britain's off-shore oil and gas rigs.

The SBS has seen action in the Oman, Borneo and the Falkland Islands War. In the latter the SBS were early ashore on South Georgia, having flown from the UK in a C-130 and then parachuted to a submarine in the South Atlantic. The submarine then took them close inshore and they then com-

Press Association

Special combat uniform with hood

Silenced Sterling SMG

Folding canvas canoe

9mm L34A1 Sterling sub-machine gun with silencer

Foresight

Above: A two-man SBS patrol coming ashore in a canvas folding canoe. They are wearing special camouflage suits and are carrying 9mm L34A1 Sterling sub-machine guns fitted with large silencers.

Left: Men of the SBS, the Royal Marines' elite unit, emerge from the hatch of a submarine during training. The ability to deliver men from a submarine onto a hostile shore is very valuable and was used on a number of occasions during the South Atlantic War of 1982.

pleted their long journey in inflatable Gemini boats. The SBS is also rumoured to have put patrols ashore on the Argentine mainland, landing from the conventional submarine, HMS *Onyx*, although this has never been confirmed. The SBS and SAS operated on the Falkland Islands long before the amphibious landings, and the SBS reconnoitred the actual landing sites at San Carlos Bay. They were there to welcome the first landing-craft to reach the shore, and also silenced the Argentinian outpost on Fanning Head, overlooking the landings. ▶

► The way in which the SBS fits in with the much larger SAS organisation is a matter for speculation, particularly as the SAS is known to have a Boat Troop, with similar equipment and capabilities to the SBS. Nevertheless, there is no known friction between the two units, and it must therefore be assumed that the responsibilities are not a problem in practice.

Selection and training

Recruitment to the SBS is from volunteers serving in the Royal Marine Commandos. All such officer and marine volunteers undergo the usual physical and psychological tests, followed by a three-week selection test. Successful candidates then go on a 15-week training course in seamanship, navigation, demolition, diving and advanced weapons handling. They then do a four-week parachute course, following which they join an operational Special Boat Section.

SBS officers and marines are not compelled to leave the SBS after a set period, as, for example, in the SAS, but like some other special forces they are usually forced to leave if they wish to obtain promotion past a certain point.

Uniforms

The SBS wear standard Royal Marine uniform and the commando green beret. The only indication in parade and barrack dress that a man belongs to the SBS is the wearing of Royal Marine parachuting wings on the right shoulder and of the "Swimmer Canoeist" badge on the right forearm. The latter has a crown above the letters "SC", flanked by laurel leaves. In parade dress both badges are embroidered in gold on a black backing. Officers of the SBS wear the wings, but not the "SC" badge (even though they are qualified to wear it by having passed the course).

Weapons and equipment

The SBS four-man patrols are usually armed with the US M16 Armalite rifle and M203 grenade launchers, although a special silenced version of the British Sterling sub-machine-gun (L34A1) is also used. Included in the patrol's equipment are plastic explosives, laser designators and burst-transmission radios. Extensive survival kits are also carried.

Boats used by the SBS include paddle-boards, specially-produced

Klepper Mark 13 collapsible boats, and the somewhat larger Gemini boats powered by 40bhp outboard motors. The SBS can also be transported by "Rigid Raider" boats, a militarised version of the glassfibre "Dory" fishing-boat, powered by outboards of up to 140bhp, and operated by the specialists of the Royal Marines' Rigid Raider Squadron.

Above: Marines of the SBS on a training exercise. Continuous experience since 1941 makes them one of the world's best trained canoe forces.

Below: 9mm L34A1 Sterling sub-machine gun, a favourite weapon of the SBS. The wooden grip is needed as the barrel casing becomes too hot to hold.

Special Air Services

In December 1975 a four-man "Active-Service Unit" of the Provisional IRA was cornered by London's Metropolitan Police in a flat in Balcombe Street, in the capital's Marylebone area. The four Irishmen held the owners—an understandably terrified couple—hostage, and the police were faced with the problem of resolving matters without physical harm coming to the elderly pair. The "Provos" were confident that they could strike a bargain with the police sooner or later. It was known that there was a radio receiver in the flat and, during a routine news broadcast, the BBC announced that an armed section of the SAS had arrived at the scene of the siege. Shortly afterwards the Provos surrendered; the police they could cope with, but the SAS—they were something else!

Foundation

The SAS was formed early in World War II, at a time when many "special" units were being raised, by Lt. David Stirling, who was then serving with No. 8 Commando, a British Army unit. Known originally as "L Detachment", by October 1942 the unit had grown to 390 men and it was redesignated 1st Special Air Service Regiment (1 SAS). After various reorganisations and a period of further growth, an SAS Brigade was formed in Scotland in January 1944, consisting of two British regiments (1 and 2 SAS), two French regiments (3 and 4 SAS), a Belgian squadron (later 5 SAS) and a signal squadron.

The SAS fought throughout the Desert campaign, in Italy and in Northwest Europe, establishing a reputation for independent action by small groups of very highly trained men, operating deep behind enemy lines. At the end of the war in Europe the British Army divested itself of "private armies" with indecent haste, and the SAS were among those to go. No. 5 SAS was handed over to the Belgian Army in September 1945, followed by 3 and 4 SAS which were transferred

to the French Army a month later. A week after this HQ SAS and 1 and 2 SAS were disbanded, and it appeared that the British Army had washed its hands of the "SAS idea", altogether and for ever.

It takes more than that to keep a good idea down, however, and within months it was decided that there would be a role for SAS-type activities in a future war in Europe. This led to the conversion of a Territorial Army (TA) unit, "The Artists' Rifles", into 21st Special Air Service Regiment (21 SAS) (Artists) —(Volunteers), the number 21 being obtained by taking the numbers of the two British wartime SAS regiments (1 and 2 SAS), combining and reversing them.

One of the early British post-war anti-colonial campaigns was the Malayan "Emergency" (1948-60). Brigadier Michael Calvert, a renowned ex-Chindit and commander of the SAS Brigade 1944-45, arrived in Malaya in 1951 and formed the "Malayan Scouts (Special Air Service)" which quickly built up to regimental size. In 1952 the Malayan Scouts were redesignated 22nd Special Air Service Regiment (22 SAS), thus marking the official return of the SAS to the regular army's order of battle. The reputation of the SAS in Malaya was second to none. They spent very long periods in the deep jungle where they established particularly close links with the aboriginal peoples, and they also pioneered the techniques for parachuting into the trees and then abseiling down long ropes to the jungle floor.

When the conflict in Malaya began to wind-down, the SAS were sent to the Oman in the Arabian peninsula in November/December 1958, where they carried out a daring attack on rebels in the 8,000ft (2,500m) high Jebel ▶

Right: An SAS trooper on patrol during the South Atlantic war. During this campaign the SAS proved that they are as good in conventional war as they are at dealing with terrorists.

"Bergen"
rucksack

Cold weather
combat hat

"Sweat rag" used
as a scarf

Belts of 7.62mm
ball ammunition

7.62mm L7A2
general-purpose
machine-gun

British Army pattern
camouflaged combat
uniform

Canvas anklets

British Army DMS
boots

▶ Akhdar, totally defeating the Arab dissidents in their own home ground. Following this success, 22 SAS moved to the UK where, after a short period in Malvern, they settled down in their now-famous home base at Bradbury Lines, Hereford. But by now they had been reduced to an HQ and two "sabre" squadrons.

The Far East soon beckoned again, however, with the "Confrontation Campaign" in Borneo, and a squadron of SAS arrived there in January 1963. Their success led to more demands for SAS and the third squadron had to be re-formed in mid-1963. This was just as well, because war broke out in Aden and from 1964-66 the three squadrons of 22 SAS were rotating between the UK, Borneo and Aden in a period known in the regiment as the "happy time". By 1967 these two wars were over and the SAS had a short period of consolidation and retraining.

In 1969 the situation in Northern Ireland suddenly exploded and the SAS began a long acquaintanceship with the Province. Simultaneously, renewed problems in Malaya and the Oman led to a return there. In July 1972, at the Battle of Mirbat in Oman, ten SAS soldiers, aided by a few local soldiers, defeated 250 dissidents in a memorable engagement. The SAS remained in the Oman for many years and there may be a few members there still. In August 1983 it was disclosed that the SAS was training a similar unit for the Sultan of Oman's "Special Force", composed of parachutists trained to exist for days on little food in desert conditions.

The anti-guerrilla campaigns of the 1950s, 1960s and early 1970s were succeeded by a new role in which the SAS quickly built up an unrivalled expertise — counter-terrorist actions. Spurred on by operations in Northern Ireland against the Irish Republican Army (IRA) and Irish National Liberation Army (INLA) the SAS has developed techniques which are copied throughout the Western world. This has led to the SAS not only being consulted by overseas governments and special forces, but

also in being directly involved in some "foreign" operations. Thus, in October 1977, two SAS men were with the West German GSG 9 unit at the attack to recapture a hijacked German airliner at Mogadishu, and SAS members were also involved in the earlier Dutch operation against the Moluccan terrorists who had taken over a train-load of hostages.

Most famous of all such episodes, however, was the London Iranian Embassy siege of May 1980 when the SAS had perforce to conduct the operation in front of the world's TV cameras. In strict compliance with English law, the Metropolitan Police conducted the operation until the terrorists murdered one of the hostages and threw his body out on the street. The police then requested the SAS to take over, and the troops stormed

Above: SAS troopers training in a desert environment. The "target" on the left is wearing the SAS sand-coloured beret and the special camouflage smock used by SAS and SBS.

in, using special weapons and tactics, and rescued all the remaining hostages. All but one of the terrorists was killed.

This spectacular success, while a god-send for the hero-hungry world media, gave the SAS far more publicity than the Service would have preferred.

By 1982 the SAS seemed to be settled in their counter-terrorist role when, to everyone's surprise, the Falklands War with Argentina broke out. No. 22 SAS were immediately involved and were given the opportunity to remind the world that they are first and foremost professional soldiers, trained for war. They spearheaded the return to South Georgia island, although the first reconnaissance landing in helicopters had to be aborted in truly appalling weather. The second landing was by inflat-

able boats and most men got ashore. One boat, however, broke down and the soldiers refused to compromise the operation by calling for help on the radio and were blown rapidly eastwards; by the greatest of good fortune they hit the very tip of the island and were later rescued by helicopter. Meanwhile, at Grytviken, squadron headquarters and one troop of D Squadron took advantage of the crippling of the Argentine submarine "Santa Fe" to rush in and overwhelm the garrison, and South Georgia was quickly back under British control. ▶

► The first SAS soldiers were ashore on East Falklands by May 1 and remained there, close to the enemy and in foul weather, for some thirty days. They provided vital intelligence on troop movements and deployments, and also targeted enemy aircraft and stores for aircraft strikes and naval gunfire support. On May 14 the SAS raided Pebble Island and blew up 11 Argentine aircraft, a reversion to their original role in the North African desert 40 years previously. It is also reported that they operated on the mainland of Argentina itself, although this has never been officially confirmed.

Their final role was to carry out a noisy and valuable diversionary attack on the eastern end of Wireless Ridge on the day before the Argentine surrender. That surrender was negotiated by Lieutenant Colonel Michael Rose, who had just handed over command of 22 SAS. He flew to Stanley to arrange the surrender terms with General Menendez and with his deep knowledge of the necessary techniques he was able to establish a total moral and psychological ascendancy over the unfortunate Argentines.

The SAS are now back to their less publicised, but scarcely routine roles, and are now probably the most famous battalion-sized unit in the world.

Organisation

The present organisation includes three regiments of approximately 600 to 700 men each. One regiment (22 SAS) is all-regular, while the other two (21 SAS (Artists Rifles) and 23 SAS) belong to the Territorial Army. There is a regular signal squadron with 22 SAS and another (63 (SAS) Signal Squadron) with the TA. These units are controlled by Director SAS Group, a brigadier whose headquarters are in London.

Although they no longer operate together the SAS maintains close links with the New Zealand Special Air Service Squadron and the Australian Special Air Service. Fraternal links are also maintained with the 1st Parachute Battalion of the Belgian Army which is descended from the wartime 5 SAS, and the Greek "Sacred Squadron (Helios Lokos)" which served with the SAS in North Africa and the Eastern Mediterranean in the last war.

There is a very close relationship between the present-day regular (22 SAS) and territorial (21 and 23 SAS) regiments. Both territorial regiments have a strong cadre of

Below: SAS trooper crossing a fence on the Brecon Beacons in Wales. Rifle is an old FN FAL used only for training (DP on the butt denotes "Drill Purpose").

Press Association

Above: Volunteers for the SAS have to show not only physical and mental ability, but also basic military skills.

regulars, who ensure that professional standards are maintained, and who pass on the benefits of recent operational experience.

Selection and training

No officer or soldier enlists directly into the regular regiment (22 SAS). Instead, volunteers come from the other regiments and corps of the British Army, which sometimes leads to the accusation that the regiment is "poaching" some of the best and most enterprising young officers and soldiers. All volunteers for the SAS must first pass the selection course, which is based at the regimental depot at Hereford. The tests take place in the Brecon area of Wales and consist of a series of tasks designed to find out whether the individual has the qualities of mental resilience, physical stamina, self-discipline and spiritual toughness which the regiment has found necessary for its missions.

The process starts with 10 days of fitness and map-reading training in groups of 20 to bring everyone up to the same basic standards. This is followed by 10 days of solitary cross-country marching, culminating in a 40 mile (64km) march in 20 hours carrying a 55lb

(25kg) Bergen rucksack. Those who have not either voluntarily or compulsorily retired now undertake 14 weeks continuation training which includes a parachute course and combat survival training. At the end of this phase the survivors are presented with their beret and badge, and are at long last members of the SAS, although the training continues with specialist courses in signalling, languages, field medicine, demolition, shooting, free-fall parachuting and other military skills. It is only after some two years that a soldier can be considered to be a fully-fledged member of the regiment, and even then there can be periods of high-intensity training for roles such as counter-revolutionary warfare commandos.

Unlike the earlier years of the SAS the emphasis today is on pulling and encouraging men to get through the tests and course, but without in any way relaxing the high standards. Nevertheless, the pass-rate is only about 20 per cent, although it must be appreciated ▶

▶ that only rarely is there any reason for any of the other 80 per cent to feel ashamed; the fact is that the SAS are, of necessity, looking for a very special combination of talents which is possessed by or can be developed in only a few people.

Once fully in the regiment the regular officers' and soldiers' normal tour of duty is three years, following which they will usually return to their parent regiment or corps. This ensures that the regiment does not become too introspective and also serves to spread around the rest of the Army that curious blend of ideas and training which constitute the SAS.

Weapons and equipment

The SAS use standard British Army small arms such as the L1A1 7.62mm Self-Loading Rifle, Brown-ing 9mm pistol and the 7.62mm General-Purpose Machine-Gun (GPMG). The Sterling 9mm machine-carbine is not used, the SAS preferring the Heckler and Kock 9mm SMG. In addition, the SAS specialise in training and using virtually any type of foreign weapon, either to take advantage of some particular attribute, or to blend in with some bit of local "scenery". Special "stun" grenades have been developed for SAS use in which the blast effect has been maximised at the expense of dam-age potential.

It was announced in March 1984 that the SAS would use two Italian-built Agusta 109 helicopters captured from the Argentinians during the Falklands War. The aircraft are now part of the Army Air Corps inventory; they can carry

The Iranian Embassy Siege April 30-May 5 1980

The siege of the Iranian Embassy in London in April—May 1980 caught the imagination of the world and brought the SAS into the limelight because the denouement took place before the gathered Press photo-graphers and TV. The eerie, black-clad figures, their efficiency and the success and sheer drama of the event established the SAS a public reputation and created an ex-pectation of success which will endure for many years.

The Iranian Embassy at No. 16 Princes Gate, London, opposite Hyde Park, was taken over at 1130 hours Wednesday April 30 by six terrorists, armed with three 9mm automatic pistols, one 0.38in revolver, two 9mm sub-machine guns and a number of Chinese-made hand-grenades. There were six men directly involved: Oan, the leader (27 years old), and five others, all in their early twenties. They were all from Arabistan, an area of Iran some 400 miles (643km) from Teheran, which had long resisted the rule of the Aryan northerners. Most had supported Ayatollah Khomeini's takeover from the Shah, only to find him as ruthless a suppressor of minorities as his predecessor. The terrorists

represented a group entitled the Democratic Revolutionary Move-ment for the Liberation of Arabistan (DRMLA), a Marxist-Leninist group based in Libya, whose cause was regional autonomy (not indepen-dence) for Arabistan.

The occupants of the Embassy at the time of the takeover num-bered 29: four British and 22 Iranian men and women, three of whom escaped during the early minutes. The terrorists' demands were initially that 91 prisoners in Arabistan be released by the Iranian authorities. The deadline was set for 1200 hours Thursday May 1, and during that night the terrorists had the first of many contacts with the London police and the media.

One sick Iranian woman was released late on the Wednesday night and a sick Englishman the following morning. The first dead-line was postponed when the police transmitted a message from ▶

Right: Two SAS men outside the Iranian Embassy in London during the brief action which ended the siege. They are aiming 9mm High-Power Browning pistols, but have a rifle and tear gas launcher ready at their feet

up to seven troops and could be equipped for many roles, including anti-tank and electronic warfare.

Uniform

The SAS deliberately shuns glamorous or flashy uniforms or embellishments, and wears standard British Army uniforms, as far as possible, with only the customary "regimental" items permitted under British practice. The three basic distinguishing marks of the SAS are the sand-coloured beret, the cap-badge (a winged dagger with the motto "Who Dares Wins") and SAS-wings worn on the right shoulder. In parade dress (No. 2 Dress) buttons, officers' Sam Browne belt, gloves and shoes are all black. Combat dress is standard British Army pattern with either the sand-coloured beret or the peaked camouflage hat with no badge. With this latter hat on there is nothing about a soldier's uniform to show that he is a member of the SAS at all. One small idiosyncracy of SAS uniform is that in "pullover order" (the popular dress worn in barracks) the rank chevrons of NCO, are worn on the shoulder straps, not on the right sleeve.

A unique combat uniform is available for use on anti-terrorist operations. This is an all-black outfit, with a black flak-vest, belt and boots. The standard issue respirator (which is made of black rubber) and grey anti-flash hood complete the outfit. Every item of this dress is worn for strictly practical reasons, but the overall effect is awe-inspiring, as was demonstrated at the Iranian Embassy siege rescue in May 1980.

London Express

▶ the terrorists to the Press, and a second deadline (1400 hours) passed without a move from either side.

By the Friday morning there had been numerous contacts between the terrorists and the police, some direct and some through inter-mediaries, but by now specific threats were being made against the lives of the hostages. Nego-tiations continued throughout the Saturday and a major advance was achieved when the terrorists agreed to release two hostages in return for a broadcast on the radio of a statement of their aims. One hostage was released in the early evening and after the statement had been broadcast on the BBC 2100 hours news, word for word as given by the terrorist leader to the police, a further hostage was released. The atmosphere in the Embassy became almost euphoric, helped by a good meal sent in by the police.

Through the Sunday the British Government discussed the situation with various Arab ambassadors, but no agreement could be reached on a possible role for them in reaching a resolution to the crisis. In the Embassy the major event in an anti-climactic day was the release of an Iranian hostage who had become very ill. On Monday the terrorists were noticeably more nervous and a shouted discussion between two British hostages and the police at noon did little to ease the tension. At about 1330 Oan's patience apparently snapped and he shot Abbas Lavasani, one of the Embassy staff, in the course of a telephone discussion with the police. This was the turning point.

Any doubts about whether any-one had actually been killed were resolved just after 1900 when the dead body was pushed through the front door of the Embassy and a pair of policemen rushed forward and carried it away on a stretcher.

SAS soldiers had visited the scene on the first day of the siege, and thereafter they stood-by in an Army barracks some two miles away. The police had obviously tried their best to identify just where the hostages and their captors were and what they were all doing, and many highly classified surveillance devices were used. The SAS were therefore as ready as it was possible to be in the circumstances when, in accordance with British legal practice, the police formally asked the military to deal with the situation.

The rescue

The plan was to use just 12 men in three teams of the customary four-man SAS groups; two teams were to take the rear, descending by rope from the roof, one team to reach the ground and the second the first-floor balcony. Both would then break-in using either frame-charges or brute force. Team three was to be at the front, crossing from a balcony at No. 15 Princes Gate to No. 16. Once inside all three teams were to rush to reach the hostages before they could be harmed.

Everything that could be done to heighten the impact of the attack was done. The 12 SAS men were dressed from head to foot in black, even including rubber anti-gas respirators, and looked extremely menacing. They would gain entrance using 4ft x 2ft (1.2 x 0.6m) frame charges, followed by stun grenades ("flash-bangs"). CS gas would also be used. The combination of explosions, noise, smoke, speed of action and the appearance of the men was all intended to strike confusion and dread into the minds of the terrorists —and succeeded brilliantly.

The SAS men had, naturally, pored over the plans of the building in minute detail and had also spent many hours studying the photo-graphs of the hostages. But, in the end—as every soldier knows—all the training and planning have to be translated into action.

At 1926 hours precisely the men of the rear attack force stepped over the edge of the roof and abseiled down. The first two went down each rope successfully, but one of the third pair became stuck, a hazard known to abseilers every-where. In the front SAS men appeared on the balcony of No. 15 and climbed over to the Embassy,

Press Association

giving the world's Press and the public an image of their regiment which will last for years.

Simultaneously the police spoke to the terrorists on the telephone and distracted their attention at the critical moment that the SAS suddenly broke in. Stun grenades exploded, lights went out and all was noise and apparent confusion. Some parts of the Embassy caught fire and the SAS man caught on the rope at the rear was cut free and dropped onto a balcony—a risk preferable to that of being roasted alive.

The SAS men swept through the Embassy. Two terrorists were quickly shot and killed. One started shooting the hostages in an upstairs

Above: The image of the SAS that shook the world. These men wear black uniforms and boots, standard respirators and NBC hoods. Their weapon is the Heckler & Koch 9mm MP5 sub-machine gun.

room, but stopped after causing a few wounds. Within minutes five of the six gunmen were dead, with the sixth sheltering among the newly-freed hostages. All survivors were rushed downstairs into the garden, where the remaining terrorist was identified and arrested. Not one hostage was killed in the attack, which was, quite simply, a major success in the West's fight against the evils of terrorism.

US Special Operations Forces

The United States has found it difficult to come to terms with Special Operations Forces (SOF). The fortunes of long-standing SOF such as the Rangers and the Special Forces have waxed and waned according to the military climate in the Pentagon and political pressures in Congress. Thus, the Rangers have been through some slim periods as have the Special Forces who almost disappeared in both the late 1950s and the late 1970s.

Further, there is a host of units involved, partly due to the sheer size of the US armed forces, but also arising from the rivalries between the individual services and the jockeying in Congress for power and influence. Thus, when in the early 1970s a special counter-terrorist unit was needed to meet the same needs as those undertaken by foreign units such as the British SAS and the West German GSG9, the only viable solution was to create something totally new— 1st Special Forces Operational Detachment— Delta—rather than adapt one of the existing bodies.

This overall situation has at last been recognised in the Pentagon by the creation on January 1, 1984, of the Joint Special Operations Agency (JSOA) to "improve the management and increase the responsiveness of these forces to the requirements of the deployed commands." Further, the individual Services have sought (or been forced) to set their own houses in order: the Army set up 1st Special Operations Command in October 1982, while the USAF has recently created 23rd Air Force to pull together its special forces commitments. It is to be hoped that these steps will lead to substantial improvements, provided, of course, these new higher-level headquarters do not lead merely to increasing bureaucracy and ossification of planning and command.

In this context the words of Major-General Joseph C. Lutz, Commanding General of US 1st Special Operations Command, are of particular interest. "In the 1st Special Operations Command we are not sitting around patting ourselves on the back because our value has apparently been recognised. On the contrary, special operations forces will never be more than modest in size. To accomplish the mission set before us, however, our soldiers must be extraordinarily professional. We are working at the

Current United States Special Forces

Service	Current Units (inc. reserves)	Proposed Enhancements
Army	**One Special Operations Command** 7 SF groups 21 SF battalions 4 Psyop groups 12 Psyop battalions	One new SF group to be formed. Increases in manpower and helicopter support.
	Two Ranger battalions	
	Civil Affairs battalion	Equipment improvement.
Navy	**Two Special Warfare Groups** 3 Special Warfare Units 2 Swimmer Delivery Vehicle Teams 5 SEAL Teams 2 Special Boat Squadrons 6 Special Boat Units	Two new SEAL teams. New specialised equipment New facilities New multi-mission boats.
Air Force	**One Special Operations Wing:** 5 squadrons **Two Reserve Special Operations Groups:** 3 squadrons **One helicopter detachment**	Additional MC-130 and HH-60D aircraft. Service life extensions for current aircraft. Avionics improvements.

Above: Most US elite units practise air-insertion operations.

business of integrating all elements of the new command into a cohesive professional force to meet any mission assigned."

The current composition of SOF and the presently promised improvements are shown in the accompanying table; it should be noted, however, that this does not include Delta, which is seeking, quite properly, to disappear into the background until it is needed again.

The USA sees the SOF as having a particularly valuable role in being the repository of knowledge and skills of low-intensity warfare (the new name for counter-insurgency or counter-revolutionary warfare). To this end SOF are specifically trained to understand this type of warfare and to be able to train the armed forces of the victims of such aggression. In Fiscal Year 1981-82, for example, 39 SOF teams carried out such missions, in nations including Somalia, Egypt, Honduras and El Salvador, while in the first nine months of 1983 36 teams assisted 12 different nations.

But this is not to deny the potential role of SOF in general war, where all forces would be involved in operations in their specialised field. Recent evidence given by the Department of Defense to Congress, for example, may be indicative of the way their thinking is developing.

"Special operations forces are one of the principal means available to us to disrupt the Soviet strategy. Here, again, we see the force multiplying effects of special operations forces. General Eisenhower reckoned that the activities of indigenous, unconventional elements operating in France were worth 15 divisions to him during the invasion of Normandy."

SOF are capable of direct action in overseas crises for which the use of other, higher profile US forces would be inappropriate. This includes hostile acts against US citizens abroad by terrorists, dissidents, or even by the foreign governments themselves. The USA has used its SOF once in this role (in public knowledge, at least)—in the attempted rescue of the US Embassy hostages in Teheran. There have been other similar operations. The first was the raid by the US Marine Corps on Koh Tang island to seek the release of the crew of the *SS Mayaguez*, and the second the pre-emptive strike in Grenada to ensure that the American medical students on the island were not used as hostages. Both were mounted at very short notice, both (although on different scales) used a considerable degree of force, and both succeeded in their aim.

One point of interest in the US SOF organisation is that the airborne units and the USMC remain outside it. Indeed, they have never spawned any major elite sub-units of their own, apart from the Marines' Force Recon. The US Navy's SEALs, for example, perform tasks which might well be thought to be a USMC responsibility and which, in other countries are performed by marines, such as the British Royal Marines Special Boat Squadron.

23rd Air Force

The 23rd Air Force is not, in the strictest sense, an "elite" unit, but its operations are so essential to the success of other US special forces that it must be included in any discussion of the subject. On March 1, 1983, all special operations forces (SOF) of the USAF were centralised under Military Airlift Command (MAC). This brought together 1st Special Operations Wing (1st SOW) at Hurlburt Field, Florida, which had previously been under Tactical Air Command (TAC), and the Aerospace Rescue and Recovery Service (ARRS), which had always been part of MAC. They are controlled by the newly created 23rd Air Force which is co-located with MAC at Scott Air Force Base, Illinois.

1st Special Operations Wing

1st SOW consists of five Special Operations Squadrons (SOS) equipped with special versions of the C-130 Hercules transport and a number of modified helicopters. Units of this wing took part in the Operation Eagle Claw (the attempted rescue of the US Embassy hostages in Teheran) as well as the Grenada rescue mission in 1983. The five squadrons are known to include 7th SOS (MC-130E), 8th

SOS (MC-130E) and 16th SOS (AC-130), but the detailed composition and organisation of 1st SOW is highly classified, though some details of their equipment are known. In 1982 this included the equipment listed below.

Lockheed AC-130A and AC-130H Hercules gunships. The wing has ten of each of these types. The AC-130A was developed for use in the Southeast Asia wars and armed with a variety of weapons ranging from Gatling guns to 105mm howitzers. The AC-130H has greater range and payload, and may have improved armament and fire control devices. In the Grenada operation AC-130Hs were reported to be firing very close to their own troops and with great accuracy.

Lockheed MC-130E and MC-130H Hercules. The wing has 13 of the -E type and ten -Hs, with a further undisclosed quantity of -Hs on order. The MC-130E is a special operations version of the C-130E, and has special avionics, an ALQ-8 ECM pod under the port wing, together with other devices to suit

Below: Near their base at Hurlburt Field, Florida, men of 1st SOW combat control team on amphibious training. They are carrying GAU-5 assault rifles.

it for low-level operations. It is used for clandestine in/exfiltration and airdrops. The MC-130H, code-named Combat Talon, is an improved -E with increased range and payload, improved command, control and communications fits, enhanced ECM equipment, and better avionics.

Sikorsky CH-3E Jolly Green Giant. This is the USAF version of the Sikorsky S-61R, and 1st SOW has six. They have armour protection, self-sealing fuel tanks, various weapons, rescue hoist, and a retractable in-flight refuelling probe.

Bell UH-1N Huey. Ten of these are held. This is a late version of the famous Huey, and is a militarised twin-engined Bell 212.

Above: Lockheed AC-130A Hercules gunship fires its 20mm Gatling guns. Note the sensor pods and covers along the fuselage side.

Below: MC-130E flying very low in rough terrain. Pilots fly their machines like fighters, even though they were built as long-range transports.

Sikorsky HH-53H Super Jolly. Nine of these large aircraft are held, optimised for special operations. In addition, 90 *Sikorsky HH-60D Night Hawks* are to be procured for the USAF, of which some are to go to 1st SOW. This is a special operations version of the UH-60 ▶

107

helicopter, optimised for the combat air rescue mission. It is equipped with terrain-following radar, forward-looking infra-red (FLIR), extra fuel, a rescue hoist, armoured protection, and an armament mix of guns and missiles.

A new helicopter—AH-X—is due to be brought into service in 1986 to improve 1st SOW's medium-lift capability.

ARRS

Like 1st SOW, ARRS is equipped with a mixture of C-130 Hercules aircraft and helicopters; indeed, it was this commonality of equipment that was one of the reasons for bringing them together. The ARRS was established on March 13, 1946, as part of Air Transport Command. In 1948 it moved to Military Air Transport Service (MATS) which in turn became MAC. The ARRS consists of some 3,800 men and women, and possesses some 210 aircraft, of which 50 are fixed-wing and the remainder helicopters. ARRS mission ranges from combat rescue through peacetime search-and-rescue to weather reconnaissance and atmospheric sampling. In its combat rescue role ARS has saved 996 lives in Korea and 2,759 in the Southeast Asia wars.

ARRS also provides recovery support for the National Aeronautics and Space Agency (NASA), starting with the Mercury series and continuing through Apollo to the current Shuttle programme. The ARRS weather reconnaissance force is composed of WC-130 aircraft which routinely locate and penetrate hurricanes and typhoons, an activity requiring the very highest degree of courage and flying skills. One curious addition to the ARRS role is the support of Strategic Air Command's (SAC) missile sites. Carried out by 37th Aerospace Rescue and Recovery Squadron at Warren AFB, Wyoming, these tasks include escorting missile

Below: USAF pilot acting as the target in a 23rd Air Force SAR training exercise in the Pacific awaits pick-up by UH-1 Huey.

convais, personnel and equipment transportation and other logistic support. Two versions of the ubiquitous C-130 deserve mention.

Lockheed HC-130H. This model was developed especially for ARRS and has extended range and a fold-out device on the nose to assist in the snatching of men or equipment from the ground, using the "sky-hook" technique. The JHC-130H has further gear to assist in the recovery of space capsules in the air.

Lockheed WC-130B and WC-130H. These models are specially fitted for weather reconnaissance.

Above: Aerospace Rescue and Recovery HC-130H retrieves package returned from space in routine recovery mission.

Uniforms

1st SOW and ARRS members wear standard USAF uniforms, but with appropriate shoulder badges. Some ARRS personnel, however, are parachute-qualified, and these men wear maroon berets and jump wings.

Below: Inside an HC-130H a 23rd Air Force SAR team prepares for a parachute jump over Alaska.

82nd Airborne Division

The US Army's only full-time parachute formation is 82nd Airborne Division, based at Fort Bragg in North Carolina. It is part of XVIII Airborne Corps, the other element of which is 101st Airborne Division (Air Assault), a 17,900-strong force, based on heliborne tactics utilising the UH-60 Black Hawk helicopter. The corps is so large it requires the XVIII Corps' 1st Corps Support Command to look after it.

The mission of 82nd Airborne Division includes as its primary task (as should every parachute formation) that of seizing from the air important ground objectives and holding them until conventional ground troops can join up and relieve them. As currently tasked, 82nd Airborne Division is at the forefront of the US Rapid Deployment Force, its unique contribution being its jump capability.

On battalion is always at 18 hours readiness to deploy, with one of its companies at 2 hours notice. This is backed up the the remainder of the Division's Ready Brigade, nearly 4,000 strong, which would follow-up within 24 hours.

The US forces can actually achieve this ambitious goal, and the 82nd is backed up by an enormous force of USAF parachute-capable aircraft, including many hundred Lockheed C-141 Star-Lifters and C-130 Hercules. The C-141s regularly display their ability to fly from the United States across the Atlantic and drop paratroops direct onto Dropping Zones (DZ) in

Below: Squad machine-gun crew with their M60. The "Airborne" flash clearly identifies them as soldiers of the elite US Army 82nd Airborne Division.

West Germany. Once committed to such an operation 82nd Airborne Division has sufficient material supplies (ammunition, rations, water and fuel) for three days at combat rates, but aerial resupply would then become essential.

A Container Delivery System (CDS) has been developed which enables a fully stocked resupply container to be delivered with great accuracy within a 109 x 437 yard (100 x 400m) area. Fixed resupply DZs are thus no longer necessary, thus absolving the ground troops from a major defensive problem which has caused great difficulties in previous parachute operations. Each CDS container can carry 20,000lb (9,072kg) of stores; C-130s can carry up to 16 and C-141s 28.

The airlift capability is improving. Stretched C-141s are now in service and the rewinging of the giant Lockheed C-5 Galaxy aircraft is well in hand. Also a future possibility is the C-17 transport, which is intended for both strategic and tactical airlift, and would include an in-flight refuelling capability, currently lacking on USAF C-130s.

Organisation

82nd Airborne Division is made up of three brigades, each of three parachute battalions, together with an integral Divisional Support Command. There are three field artillery battalions, each with eighteen 105mm towed howitzers. The divisional tank battalion has 54 M551 Sheridan armoured reconnaissance vehicles, which have the great advantage of being airdroppable. They have not been an outstanding success in US Army service, however, nor could they ▶

Above: US Army paratrooper has his equipment checked prior to making a jump on Exercise Bright Star '83. Main parachute is on his back, reserve in front.

Above right: Men of 82nd Airborne Division moving off from Salines Airfield, Grenada. This successful undertaking has raised morale in all US forces.

▶ provide the airborne division with a genuine anti-armour capability.

Aviation support integral to 82nd Airborne Division is considerable. This includes 48 AH-1S Cobras armed with TOW missiles, 90 UH-1H Huey transport helicopters (to be replaced by Black Hawk UH-60s) and 59 OH-58 Kiowa reconnaissance helicopters.

Selection and training

Soldiers can enter the US airborne forces direct, but must pass a rigorous selection, training and parachute course before being a full member of the division. Training of the units within the division is particularly intense and the three brigades rotate through a three-cycles-per-quarter system. There is also a host of exercises ranging from divisional down to company level, all aimed at keeping the fighting edge of the units razor sharp. Every soldier and officer, including women, in the division must be (and remain) parachute qualified, the standard equipment currently being the MC1-1B steerable 'chute.

Weapons and equipment

Crucial to the equipment policy of the division is the tactical concept, which is based upon the Airborne Anti-Armour Defence (AAAD). Terrain, coupled with natural and man-made obstacles, is used to create "islands" of mutually-supporting anti-armour weapon teams, supported, of course, by artillery and close air support. Enemy armour would be canalised into killing zones where they would be destroyed piecemeal from the flanks and rear.

This concept requires an anti-tank system capable of air delivery and with effective ranges out to 3,280 yards (3,000m). There is also a requirement for integral air support and for an armoured counter-attack force. Any sophisticated enemy can also be expected to throw considerable air assets at any major airborne landing, making air ▶

Right: Paratroopers of 82nd Airborne Division boarding a C-130. This fine aircraft is one of the best para mounts ever, although not the greatest!

▶ defence a major requirement for the 82nd.

To meet these needs 82nd Airborne Division is equipped with light, effective weapons systems, although most of it is standard Army issue, and there is nothing like the range of specially developed equipment available to the Soviet airborne forces. Main anti-armour weapon is the highly effective TOW crew-served missile system, backed up by the M47 Dragon, and Light Anti-tank Weapon (LAW), both of which are shoulder-launched.

The M551 Sheridan soldiers on in 82nd, but is overdue for replacement by a more satisfactory system. This is a major deficiency area, as any large airborne force is at its most vulnerable in the early few days of deployment, especially from armoured attack. Anti-tank systems such as TOW can go part of the way to meeting the requirement, but a mobile reserve striking force is essential, and this is currently lacking.

As described above there is a large helicopter component in the division and the AH-1S could be expected to make a significant addition to the anti-tank capability. For air defence the division is armed with 48 six-barrel Gatlings (the Vulcan system) on wheeled mounts, backed up by Stinger, a man-portable shoulder-launched missile.

Uniforms

The uniforms and insignia of the 82nd Airborne Division are remarkably conventional. Normal US Army camouflage combat uniforms are worn, with the standard helmet. "Subdued" rank and qualification badges are worn, together with the "AA" (All-American) divisional patch on the left sleeve. A maroon beret is now being worn again, having been discontinued in the years 1978-80, greatly to the indignation of the airborne officers and soldiers.

Left: Exercise Bright Star '83 included combined drops by paratroops of 82nd Airborne Division and the Egyptian Army. Upper C-130 is Egyptian, while lower aircraft is a USAF MC-130E

Delta

US Army Colonel Charles Beckwith served with the British SAS in 1962-63 and on his return to the US Army sought to form a unit with the same organisation, ideals and functions as the SAS. After numerous attempts spread over many years he succeeded, and the new force—named 1st Special Forces Operational Detachment-Delta (Delta, for short)—was authorised on November 19, 1977. This unit should not be confused with the Delta Project (Detachment B-52) set up by the Special Forces in Vietnam in the mid-1960s (and at one time commanded by Beckwith), which was a totally different organisation and concept.

The prime role of Delta was to deal with terrorist incidents affecting US interests, a very topical requirement in the light of the rash of such incidents at that time, such as the Munich Olympic Games hostage incident (August 1972) and the Mogadishu rescue operation by GSG 9 (October 1977).

Following its setting up, Delta proceeded to select and train its men, and various unit tasks were successfully undertaken. Then, on November 4, 1979, Iranian "students" broke into the US Embassy in Teheran, taking all the staff hostage, and from then on Delta was increasingly deeply involved in planning a rescue operation, culminating in the actual attempt on April 24/25, 1980.

Organisation

Following the SAS pattern, Delta itself is divided into squadrons, which in turn are sub-divided into troops. The troops are 16 men strong, capable of operating either as a troop, or in two groups of eight, four groups of four, or eight groups of two. In its early stages there was only one squadron (A Squadron) but this split into two, forming B Squadron, in early 1979.

After the failure of the Teheran rescue operation a top-level re- ▶

Left: US Army officer from Special Forces Project Delta in South Vietnam. Colonel Beckwith was with this unit 1965-66 and founded the quite separate 1st Special Forces Operational Detachment-Delta in 1977.

Above: US SOF trooper (unknown unit) armed with Czech 7.62mm Model 58P rifle. Many elite units specialise in training on foreign small arms, which may be captured on operations and used for deception purposes.

▶ assessment was undertaken. Its report made a series of recommendations, and it is to be assumed that those affecting the organisation of the USA's counter-terrorist forces have been implemented. These were:

"*Recommendation.* It is recommended that a Counter-terrorist Joint Task Force (CTJTF) be established as a field agency of the Joint Chiefs of Staff with permanently assigned staff personnel and certain assigned forces.

"*Mission.* The CTJTF, as directed by the National Command Authority (NCA), through the Joint Chiefs of Staff, would plan, train for, and conduct operations to counter terrorist activities directed against the United States interests, citizens and/or property outside the United States.

"*Concept.* The CTJTF would be designed to provide the NCA with a range of options utilizing US military forces in countering terrorist acts. Such forces might range from a small force of highly trained specialized personnel to a larger joint force.

"*Relationships.* The Commander, CTJTF (COMCTJTF), would be responsible directly to the Joint Chiefs of Staff. The CTJTF staff should be filled with individuals of all four Services, selected on the basis of their specialized capabilities in the field of special operations of various types.

"*Forces.* The organic forces permanently assigned to the JTF should be small and limited to those which have a unique capability in special operations."

It would seem a safe assumption that Delta is at the heart of those permanently assigned forces with such a "unique capability".

Selection and training

While under Colonel Beckwith's command Delta's selection and training processes were essentially similar to those used by the SAS. Since he handed over command these processes will doubtless have been refined by the new commanding-officer, but will probably be fundamentally unaltered. Selection courses will have the accent on individual qualities and potential, but weeding out the "gung-ho" adventurist, who is as much a ▶

Right: A Delta trooper at Desert One. His jacket has a US flag covered by a patch which would have been ripped off at the Embassy.

Below: RH-53D helicopters on board USS *Nimitz* training for the Teheran rescue, Delta's most public test so far, which failed through no fault of Delta's.

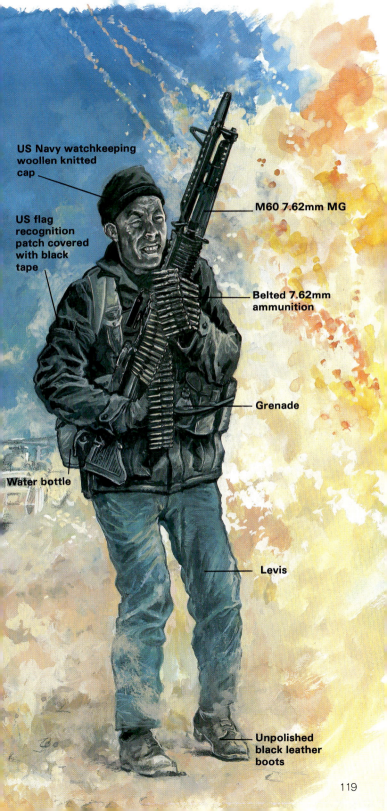

US Navy watchkeeping
woollen knitted
cap

US flag
recognition
patch covered
with black
tape

M60 7.62mm MG

Belted 7.62mm
ammunition

Grenade

Water bottle

Levis

Unpolished
black leather
boots

119

▶ menace to his comrades as he is to himself. Very high shooting standards are set; for example, snipers must achieve 100 per cent shots on target at 600 yards (548m) and 90 per cent at 1,000 yards (914m). Much use is made of the "shooting house" in training men to deal with terrorists in buildings and aircraft cabins, to ensure that the terrorists and not hostages are killed.

Weapons and equipment

Very little is known of Delta's equipment and weapons, although clearly they will be able to get most of what the most technologically advanced country in the world can provide. It is certainly known that their snipers use the Remington

Operation Eagle Claw Rescue attempt in Iran, 1980

On November 4, 1979 a group of Iranian "students" poured into the US Embassy compound in Teheran and held the 53 occupants hostage for the ensuing months, plus a further three in the Foreign Ministry. From the earliest days of the crisis one of the options under constant review and development was a military rescue, although both diplomatic and military endeavours were constantly bedevilled by the continuing chaos in Iran, the uncertain ever-changing intentions of the captors, and the vacillating position of the Iranian leadership. An unchanging factor was the remoteness of Teheran from available US bases. The plan that was eventually decided upon centred on Colonel Beckwith and Delta, although it obviously involved many more both directly and indirectly. The overall codename was Operation Eagle Claw, while the helicopter element was designated Operation Evening Light.

The plan

The plan was relatively simple, complicated mainly by the problems of time and space, and comprised some preliminary moves and a three-phase operation.

Preliminary moves. In the preliminary moves Delta was to fly, via Germany and Egypt, to Masirah airfield in Oman. There they would transfer to C-130s and, flying at very low level to avoid the radar, cross the Gulf of Oman and southern Iran to land at Desert One, a remote site in the Dasht-e-Karir Salt Desert, 265 nautical miles (490km) south east of Teheran. Meanwhile, eight US Navy RH-53D helicopters, which had

been deployed some weeks earlier via Diego Garcia would take off from the USS *Nimitz* and, flown (also at very low level) by their US Marine Corps crews, join up with the main party at Desert One.

Phase I: Insertion. At Desert One the plan was for the six C-130s (three troop carriers; three to refuel the helicopters) to land and await the helicopters, who were scheduled to arrive some 30 minutes later. Because Desert One was beside a road (judged to be little used) a 12-strong Road Watch Team was the first to deploy to intercept and detain any passing Iranians. When they had refuelled the helicopters were to load the assault team and fly on towards Teheran, dropping off the men at a landing-zone and then proceeding to their helicopter hide some 15 miles (24km) to the north. The assault group was to be met by two agents at the landing zone and guided by them to a remote wadi, some 5 miles away (8km). Helicopters and men would then rest in their hides through the day.

Phase IIA: The rescue. After last light one agent would take the 12 drivers/translators to collect six Mercedes trucks, while the other agent would take Colonel Beckwith on a route reconnaissance. At 2030 hours the complete unit would embus at the hide and drive to Teheran, the actual rescue operation starting between 2300 and 2400 hours. Having disposed of the guards and released the hostages, it was planned to call in the helicopters, either to the embassy compound if an LZ could be cleared (the students had erected poles to prevent a surprise landing)

40XB rifle with 12x Redfield telescopic sights, and for the Teheran operation two out of three machine-gunners were armed with M60s while the third had a Heckler and Koch HK21.

For units such as Delta, which may have to operate outside their own country and in remote areas, communications are obviously critical. According to Colonel Beckwith's account, on the Teheran operation he had man-portable satellite ground terminals which enabled him to communicate from Desert One (see Operation Eagle Claw, which follows) back to Washington, and would have also given him links between the various "hide locations" within Iran.

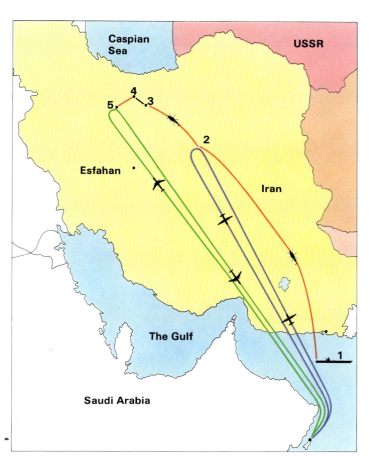

or, if this was impracticable, to a nearby football stadium. Once all the hostages were clear the assault party would be taken out by helicopter, the White Element (see table) being the last out.
Phase IIB: Rescue at the Foreign Ministry. Concurrently with Phase IIA the 13-man special team would assault the Foreign Ministry, rescue ▶

Above: The Eagle Claw plan was for helicopters (red) to fly from USS *Nimitz* (1) to Desert One (2), pick up Delta, flown in by C-130 (blue), then fly to hides (3) near Teheran (4). Helicopters would take the freed hostages to an airstrip (5) held by US Rangers. They would then fly out in C-141s (green).

▶ the hostages there, and take them to an adjacent park where they would all be picked up by a helicopter.

Phase III: Extraction. While the action was taking place in Teheran a Ranger contingent would seize Manzarieh airfield, some 35 miles (56km) to the south, and several C-141 turbojet transports would fly in. Once everyone had been evacuated from Teheran to Manzarieh they would be flown out in the C-141s, the Rangers leaving last. All surviving helicopters would be abandoned at Manzarieh.

Contingency plans. Various contingencies were foreseen and plans made accordingly; for example, in the event that not enough helicopters were available to lift everyone out of Teheran in one lift. One critically important condition had been agreed throughout the planning, namely that there had to be an absolute minimum of six helicopters to fly out of Desert One.

Command and control. The ground force commander was Colonel Beckwith, who reported to Major-General James Vaught, the Commander Joint Task Force (COMJTF) who was at Wadi Kena airfield in Egypt; they were linked by portable satellite systems. General Vaught had a similar link back to Washington, DC, where General David Jones, the Chairman of the Joint Chiefs of Staff, was in session with President Jimmy Carter throughout

the critical hours of the operation. In a last-minute change of plans Air Force Colonel James Kyle was appointed commander at Desert One.

Operation Eagle Claw: Ground Personnel

Group	Strength	Origin	Task

Main Assault Group:
  Red Element
  Blue Element
  White Element
	
	40
	40
	13
		
		Delta
			Secure Western end of compound.
			Secure Eastern sector of Embassy.
			Secure Roosevelt Avenue during main action, then cover withdrawal to football stadium.

Foreign Ministry Assault Team	13	Special Forces unit	Rescue 3 hostages held in Foreign Ministry building in Teheran.
Road Watch Team	12	Rangers	Mostly Rangers, but with some Delta soldiers.
Driving Team	12	Volunteers	6 drivers; 6 assistants/interpreters.
Iranian general	2	—	General on-site assistance
DoD Agents	4	—	Positioned in Teheran prior to operation; organise/act as guides.
Manzarieh Airfield Defence Team	Company	Rangers	Take and hold airfield for fly-out.
Commander Joint Task Force (COMJTF)	?	?	Located at Wadi Kena, Egypt, then fly to Manzarieh during evacuation phase.

Execution

The C-141 airlift of the ground party from the USA to Masirah went according to plan, as did the C-130 flights to Desert One. The ▶

Above: RH-53Ds are readied for Eagle Claw. Optimised for mine-sweeping, the RH-53D had good range and payload and was shipboard compatible.

Operation Eagle Claw: Aircraft

Aircraft	Type	Number	Tasks
MC-130E Hercules	Special operations aircraft with special avionics fit.	3	Fly men and stores from Masirah to Desert One. Two to return to Masirah at once (empty), the third to wait for Road Watch Team.
EC-130E Hercules	Command and control conversion of C-130	3	Carry fuel from Masirah to Desert One to refuel helicopters.
RH-53D Sea Stallion	Minesweeping version of H-53 helicopter, selected because of its combination of range, payload, shipboard compatibility and security considerations.	8	Fly empty from USS *Nimitz* to Desert One. Pick up men and stores, fly them to hide site, then go to separate helicopter hide. Next night fly to Teheran, extract hostages/rescue force and take to Mansarieh.
AC-130E Hercules	Specialised "gunship" version of C-130.	4	One over Teheran to prevent Iranian reinforcements reaching embassy. One over Teheran airfield to prevent Iranian aircraft taking off. Two reserves.
C-141 Starlifter	Military transport aircraft	3	Fly into Manzarieh to extract whole force on completion of operation.
C-130 Hercules	Military tactical transport	3(?)	Fly Ranger company into Manzarieh to take and hold airfield.

▶ first aircraft, carrying Colonels Beckwith and Kyle, Blue Element and the Road Watch Team, landed safely and the Road Watch Team deployed, immediately having to stop a bus containing 45 people who were detained under guard. Minutes later two more vehicles appeared from the south; the first, a petrol tanker, was hit by an anti-tank rocket and burst into flames, but the driver escaped in the second vehicle which drove off at high speed. The first C-130 then took off, leaving those on the ground briefly on their own. The second C-130 then came in and unloaded and, after the remaining four C-130s had landed, took off again for Masirah. The four C-130s and the ground party then waited for the helicopters—and waited.

The helicopters were, quite literally, the key to the operation. The eight helicopters had taken off from *USS Nimitz* (some 50 miles off the Iranian coast) at 1930 hours (local) and headed north for Desert One. At about 2145 hours helicopter No 6 indicated an impending catastrophic blade failure, one of the two really critical problems requiring an abort. The crew landed, confirmed the prob-lem, removed sensitive documents and were then picked up by heli-copter No 8 which then followed the other some minutes behind.

About one hour later the leading RH-53Ds ran into a very severe and totally unexpected dust storm; all emerged from this, flew on for an hour and then encountered a second and even worse dust storm. The helicopter force commander— Major Seiffert, USMC—had earlier lost his inertial navigation system and, entirely blinded, flew back out of the first dust storm and landed, accompanied by helicopter No. 2. Major Seiffert had a secure radio link to COMJTF, who told him that the weather at Desert One was clear; consequently, after some 20 minutes on the ground both aircraft took off again and followed the others to Desert One.

Meanwhile, helicopter No. 5 suffered a major electrical failure and lost most instruments. With no artificial horizon or heading, and with mountains ahead, he was compelled to abort, and returned to the *Nimitz;* thus leaving six helicopters to continue the mission.

The first helicopter (No. 3) cleared the dust storm some 30nm (56km) from Desert One and,

using the burning Iranian petrol tanker as a beacon, landed some 50 minutes late. The remaining aircraft straggled in over the next half-an-hour, all coming from different directions (except Nos. 1 and 2, which were together). The crews were very shaken by their experience, but the helicopters were quickly moved to their tanker C-130s, refuelling began, and the assault party started to board their designated aircraft.

Colonel Beckwith was fretting on the ground, 90 minutes behind schedule when he was informed that helicopter No. 2 had had a partial hydraulic failure during the flight; the pilot had continued to Desert One in the hope of effecting repairs, but these proved impossible. After a quick discussion, Colonel Kyle spoke to General Vaught in Egypt, who countered with a suggestion that they continue with five, despite the agreed plan that six was the absolute minimum.

The decision to call the whole thing off was quickly reached, however, although whether it was made at Desert One or in far-off Washington has never been clearly established. But there was no problem in aborting at this stage, the only minor complication being that helicopter No. 4, which had been on the ground longest, needed to top up with fuel before setting off to the *Nimitz*. Only one C-130 had enough fuel left and to clear a space for No. 4 helicopter No. 3 took off and banked to the left, but, because of the height (5,000ft/ 1,525m) and its weight (42,000lb/ 19,050kg), it could not maintain the hover and slid back straight into the C-130. It was just 0240 hours.

The effect was instantaneous and disastrous: both aircraft exploded, debris flew around and ammunition began to cook off. Five USAF aircrewmen in the C-130 and three marines in the RH-53D died, but 64 Delta men inside the C-130 escaped quickly from the aircraft and rescued the loadmaster. The decision was then made to abandon the remaining helicopters and the whole party returned to Masirah in the three C-130s.

Below: RH-53D helicopters flying in formation before the raid. They were both the key to success and the ultimate cause of the operation's failure.

Rangers

General Creighton Abrams, former US Army chief of Staff, described the Rangers as follows: "The Ranger battalion is to be an elite, light and the most proficient infantry battalion in the world, a battalion that can do things with its hands and weapons better than anyone. Wherever the Ranger battalion goes, it is apparent that it is the best."

The United States Army has two battalions of Rangers. Officially they are the 1st and 2nd Battalions of the 75th Infantry Regiment (1/75 and 2/75), but they are more popularly known as the First and Second Ranger Battalions. 1/75 is based in south-east USA at Fort Stewart, Georgia, while 2/75 is at Fort Lewis in Washington State. A third battalion (3/75 Infantry) will be activated in late 1984 at Fort Benning, Georgia. The US Army Rangers are the spiritual descendants of the old Indian fighters led by Major Robert Rogers in the pre-revolutionary colonial army, a tradition which was revived in World War II by Merril's Marauders in Burma and by Darby's Rangers in Europe. The latter, long forgotten force comprised six battalions which were raised and trained in the USA, and which fought with distinction in Sicily and Italy. Ranger units remained in the US Army's order of battle until the end of the Korean War, when they were quietly disbanded, and most of their tasks were picked up by the Special Forces.

In the post-Vietnam trauma the Special Forces were reduced drastically, and devoted most of their energies to a simple fight for survival. The Ranger School had been operating for many years to maintain a good standard of leadership in the Army and in 1975 it was decided that two Ranger battalions should be re-formed, to perform a number of unique missions.

The Rangers were earmarked to take part in the Iranian hostages rescue mission and were about to fly into Iran when the mission was cancelled due to the disaster of Desert One (see entry on "Special Forces"). Their first operational opportunity did not, therefore, arise until the Grenada operation in 1982, when they spearheaded the landing on Port Malines airfield.

In general war the Rangers' tasks include deep reconnaissance into enemy territory, strategic raids, ambushes and other high-priority missions. Peacetime tasks include raids requiring special expertise, particularly in the anti-terrorist field.

Below: US Army Rangers of 75th Infantry Regiment on patrol in swamp country. They are armed with the M16A1 rifle; note how the nearest soldier has two magazines taped together to give rapid change-over in action.

Organisation

The two Ranger battalions reported direct to Forces Command, but in October 1982 became part of the newly-created 1st Special Operations Command, which has its headquarters at Fort Bragg. 1/75 and 2/75 have a conventional organisation of three companies and an HQ company, with a total unit strength of 606 men. Among attached specialists are three teams from the USAF, each of a Forward Air Controller (FAC) and a radio operator. (These men are airborne qualified, but surprisingly do not have to attend the Ranger course.)

All men in the two battalions are volunteers and come from other units of the Army. They do a standard two year tour, which can be extended by six months, subject to a recommendation by the commanding officer.

Weapons and equipment

1/75 and 2/75 are equipped as light infantry battalions, and the heaviest weapon is the 90mm recoilless rifle. Squads are armed with an M60 MG, M203 grenade

Above: Ranger carrying M16A1 rifle fitted with M203 grenade launcher below the barrel. Sight for firing the grenade is above barrel. Range 440yd (400m).

launcher, and the balance with M16A1 rifles. Company headquarters include a M224 60mm mortar. Some individuals such as radio operators, senior NCOs and officers carry the CAR-15 short-barrelled weapon. All ranks are trained on foreign weapons, especially those of the Warsaw Pact and NATO.

Selection and training

Volunteers for the Ranger battalions must be airborne qualified, and many go straight from the Ranger School course. Attendance at that course is not a prerequisite, however, and young soldiers can go direct to the Ranger Indoctrination Program (ominously abbreviated to "RIP"), which is three weeks long. This starts with physical (including swimming) tests, and some eight parachute jumps from a CH-47.

▶

▶ The course concentrates on basic military skills and brings weapon-handling and infantry tactics up to a very high standard. The students are deliberately put under considerable stress. Courses are usually about 30 strong (minimum is 10) and an average of some 70 per cent pass and go on to one of the battalions. Those who have not already done so will normally go on the Ranger School course after some 6 to 9 months in the unit; their pass rate is very high.

The two battalions have a very arduous training schedule, and divide their year into two 5½-month periods, separated by two-week block leaves. Training exercises are conducted all over the USA, and abroad wherever possible, with the particular aim of finding different climates and environments.

The US Army's Ranger School is an unusual institution. It has existed for many years, even when there were no Ranger units as such, with the aim of training officers and

Rescue in Grenada October 25 1983

Following the inglorious end of the Vietnam War, American forces tried to keep a low profile on the international scene. Two rescue operations were attempted in efforts to secure the release of the crew of the *Mayaguez* and the Iranian embassy hostages. US troops also took part in various peacekeeping forces such as those

in the Sinai and in Beirut. However, major use of force was eschewed for both international and domestic reasons.

But in October 1983 President Reagan decided that the United States should join with six Caribbean states in the invasion of the island of Grenada "to restore peace, order and respect for human rights;

NCOs. The whole gamut of "Ranger skills" is taught, including land navigation, patrolling, weapon handling, hand-to-hand combat, survival, and mountaineering. The under-lying purpose of the course, however, is to improve the standards of self-confidence and leadership throughout the army as whole (a few students also attend from the USAF and USMC). The course consists of three-week modules and those who pass can wear the Ranger flash.

Uniform

Dress is standard US Army uniform, with standard badges and embellishments. Those who wear the "Ranger" flash on their right sleeve do so because they have passed Ranger School and not because they are in a Ranger unit. Trainees wear jungle fatigues and the patrol hat during training, while qualified members of the battalions wear camouflage suits. The only obvious item of Ranger dress is the black beret with the Ranger badge.

to evacuate those who wish to leave; and to help the Grenadians re-establish governmental institutions." On October 19, Grenada's Prime Minister, Maurice Bishop and several Cabinet members and labour leaders had been murdered by their former military associates, and a Revolutionary Military Council had later been announced, amid

Left: Grenada is a tiny island in the Caribbean but the USA was determined that it would not be another Cuba.

Below: US Rangers move off from Port Salines airfield, Grenada. It was a short, sharp campaign, lasting from October 25 to November 2, 1983, during which surprise played a major part in its undoubted success.

rumours that other government members had been murdered. US Intelligence reported Soviet/Cuban backing for the revolutionary regime, with Cubans actually establishing on the island new fortifications, arms caches and military communications.

President Regan viewed Grenada as "a Soviet-Cuban colony being readied as a major military bastion to export and undermine democracy." Uppermost in his mind was the position of some 1,000 US citizens, and especially the 600-odd young Americans at a medical school near the Port Salines airfield. The prospect of these youngsters being held hostage by the Marxist government was very serious and would have provided a far worse crisis than even that of the Iranian embassy staff. ▶

▶ Information on the resisting troops and their dispositions in Grenada seem to have been fairly sparse, but the US forces had three immediate objectives within the overall mission of the total capture of the whole island and the restoration of a democratic government. These three tasks were the freeing of the 600 medical students, the release of the governor (Sir Paul Scoones) and the defeat of the Cuban troops on the island. US Navy Seals were responsible for capturing the governor's residence, and Marines for the Pearls Airport on the island's east coast. The crucial task was, however, the taking of Port Salines airfield, which was being constructed and guarded by Cubans. This task was given to the Rangers.

Execution

The Marine assault on Pearls Airport began at 0500 hours (local) on October 25, while H-hour for the Rangers was 0536. The Rangers left the staging airfield on Barbados in the early hours aboard MC-130E Hercules aircraft of 8th Special Operations Squadron, 1st Special Operations Wing, USAF, based at Hurlburt Field in Florida. These aircraft were accompanied by AC-130 Hercules gunships (the famous "Spectres" of the Vietnam war) of 16th Special Operations Squadron.

As they came in over Port Salines searchlights were suddenly switched on, which quickly found the lumbering C-130s team and enabled the anti-aircraft guns to open up on both the aircraft and the descending parachutists. The AC-130s were quickly called into action and silenced most of the Cuban guns. Among the lead elements in the assault was a 12-man team from the 317th Tactical Airlift Wing responsible for combat control of the drop, and these were quickly inside the air traffic control building.

Once on the ground the Rangers, told to expect some 500 Cubans (350 "workers" and a "small" military advisory team) found themselves under attack from some 600 well armed professional soldiers. The Cubans were armed with mortars and machine-guns, and had at least six armoured personnel carriers. A brisk battle developed in which the Rangers quickly gained the upper hand, and

Right: Men of 2/75th Rangers receive the Combat Infantry badge on return from Grenada.

Below: The US DoD released this photo to show the Soviet influence on Grenada.

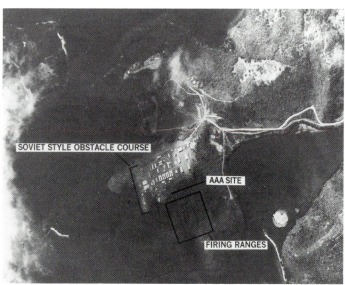

SOVIET STYLE OBSTACLE COURSE

AAA SITE

FIRING RANGES

by 0700 they were in complete control. The runway was cleared of obstacles (boulders, vehicles, pipes) and at 0715 the first C-130 of the second wave was able to land with reinforcements.

The Rangers then moved out, heading for the medical campus; brushing aside snipers and scattered resistance, they reached their objective by 0830 hours, to be greeted by some very relieved students. This campus—the True Blue medical college—was secured by 0850, although the other medical school at Grand Anse was not liberated until the following day by airborne troops.

Assessment

Which Ranger battalion took part has still not been announced publicly, although, in view of the haste with which the operation was mounted, it would seem that only the 1/75 in nearby Georgia could have reached the Caribbean in time. The Rangers played their part very well. They led the assault on the airfield, against considerable resistance, secured their initial objective and went on to achieve the second all in just under 3½ hours. In fact, the whole Grenada operation was mounted so swiftly that no national or international opposition could be mobilised to resist it, and the actual attack, even though it took longer than anticipated, was over before anything more dangerous than words could be aimed at President Reagan and the US Administration. It was a real military success, and one in which the Rangers acquitted themselves well, as usual.

Special Forces

Like the British Special Air Service (SAS) the Special Forces of the United States Army trace their short, but eventful history back to World War II. During a visit to the United Kingdom, General George C. Marshall, then the US Army's Chief of Staff, received a briefing from the energetic and persuasive Vice-Admiral Lord Louis Mountbatten, the British Chief of Combined Operations. The led General Marshall to authorise the raising of a combined Canadian and American unit—the 1st Special Service Force—whose task would be raids and strikes.

This unique force comprised three regiments of two battalions each. The men were trained in demolitions, rock-climbing, amphibious assault, skiing and parachuting, and they fought in the Aleutians, North Africa, Italy and Southern France. As with other special forces, the Special Service Force was disbanded with unseemly haste in the final days of the war in Europe.

Again reflecting what was happening in the British Army, the Special Forces were resuscitated in the early 1950s, with 10th Special Forces Group being activated at Ford Bragg, North Carolina on June 20, 1952, followed by 77th Special Forces Group on September 25, 1953. (The numbering appears to have been entirely at random.) These were followed by 1st Special Forces Group, which was raised on June 24, 1957 in Okinawa. This group sent a small team to train 58 men of the South Vietnamese Army at Nha Trang during this year, beginning a long association between the Special Forces and the Republic of Vietnam. Next, 5th Special Forces Group was raised on September 21, 1961, initially at Fort Bragg, but later it moved to Vietnam and became responsible for all Special Forces activities in that country.

President Kennedy became fascinated with the Special Forces and visited Fort Bragg in the autumn of 1961, where he authorised the wearing of the distinctive and symbolical headress—the green beret. Also as a result of this visit, the first troops of the Special Forces deployed to South Vietnam in November 1961.

Below: Special Forces training is rigorous and constant, and takes place at specially constructed courses at Army bases, such as this one at Fort Bragg, as well as "in the field" in a variety of terrains from desert to snow-covered mountains.

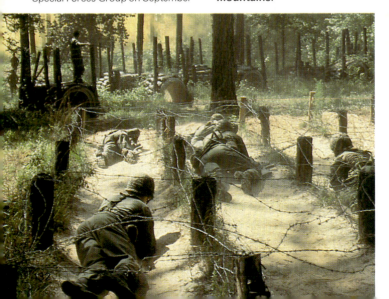

The original idea when the Special Forces were raised in the 1950s was that they would wage guerrilla operations against regular enemy troops in a conventional war. It soon became clear, however, that in Vietnam the enemy himself was a guerrilla and so the Special Forces had to revise their methods. One of the principal programmes was the raising and training of Civilian Irregular Defense Groups (CIDG), with more than 80 CIDG camps being set up in the years 1961-65.

Above: A patrol of the US Army's Special Forces in close-country. After a post-Vietnam period of neglect the Special Forces (the "Green Berets") are now in vogue once again. A new HQ has been set up, new units formed and equipment bought, all spurred by events in Latin America.

The Special Forces eventually operated throughout South Vietnam in a variety of roles, only some of which have so far been revealed. They probably had more dealings

with the ARVN (South Vietnamese Army) and with the minority peoples than had any other element of the US forces, and they received many awards for heroism and for dedication to duty. Despite this, their relationship with some elements of the US chain-of-command was not always easy, with mistrust and suspicion sometimes interfering with their operations. This is all too frequently a problem for such elite forces of most nationalities. The last soldier of the Special Forces left South Vietnam on March 1, 1971.

The Special Forces have always operated throughout the US areas of responsibility. An early deployment was to Bad Tolz in Bavaria, in the US Zone of the Federal Republic of Germany. Other groups operate in the Panama Canal Zone. Special Forces have long been involved in "advising" friendly armies in Asia, Africa, and (particularly) Latin America. They have thus tended to be always just on the edge of the limelight, occasionally being exposed by the media as, for example, recently in Latin America. Nevertheless, they are now very firmly a part of the US Army's order of battle and likely to remain there for a very long time.

Above: A Group of Special Forces soldiers on a training exercise. The lead scout is carrying a 5.56mm Colt Commando, derived from the M16 but with a shorter barrel, larger flash suppressor and a telescopic butt. Only the Green Berets use this gun.

Organisation

There are currently seven known Special Forces Groups. 5th SFG (Airborne); Fort Bragg (Active Army). 7th SFG (Airborne); Fort Bragg (Active Army). 10th SFG (Airborne); Fort Devens, Mass (Active Army). 11th SFG (Airborne); Fort Mead, Md (Army Reserve). 12th SFG (Airborne); Arlington Heights, I11 (Army Reserve). 19th SFG (Airborne); Salt Lake City, Utah (National Guard). 20th SFG (Airborne); Birmingham, Ala (National Guard). Bn/10th SFG (Airborne); Bad Tolz, Germany. 3Bn/7th; Canal Zone, Panama.

In addition to these it was announced by Secretary of Defense Weinberger in 1983 that a further group headquarters and two Special Forces battalions will be raised in Fiscal Year 1984. He also announced that a new overall headquarters — 1st Special Opera-

Organisation of Special Forces "A Team"

Commanding Officer:	Captain.
Executive Officer:	Lieutenant.
Operations Sergeant:	Sergeant (E8).
Heavy Weapons Leader:	Sergeant (E7).
Intelligence Sergeant:	Sergeant (E7).
Light Weapons Leader:	Sergeant (E7).
Medical Specialist:	Sergeant (E7).
Radio Supervisor:	Sergeant (E7).
Engineer Sergeant:	Sergeant (E7).
Assistant Medical Specialist:	Sergeant (E6).
Chief of Research and Development:	Sergeant (E5).
Engineer:	Sergeant (E5).

NOTE:
In the US Army ranks are graded from E1 (the lowest) upwards. E5 to E8 are grades within the rank of sergeant (British equivalents would be approximately: E5/6=corporal; E7=sergeant; E8=staff-sergeant).

tions Command—had recently been formed, with the task of consolidating the management of all SOF assets.

The traditional organisation pattern of the Special Forces has been based on the Operations Detachment A, more popularly known as an "A Team". This is 12 strong, as shown in the table.

Four A Teams are commanded by a B Team, commanded by a major, with a further 5 officers and 18 soldiers. A Special Forces company is commanded by a lieutenant

Above: Special Forces "A Team" coming ashore on a training exercise. The main role of the Special Forces is the development of resistance behind enemy lines and a 12-man "A Team" is capable of organising, equipping and training a battalion-size guerrilla force of 650 men.

colonel and comprises an administrative detachment, and an Operations Detachment Type C which is made up of three B Teams.

▶ Selection and training

All officers and soldiers in the Special Forces must be airborne qualified, and many are also trained in free-fall parachuting and/or for swimming roles. All soldiers must also have at least two special-isations, eg, engineering, Intelli-gence, weapons, communications, demolitions. Many must also be trained in foreign languages.

The training for the Special Forces is both thorough and tough. Further, like many Western special troops they will frequently attend courses with other armies.

Weapons and equipment

The US Special Forces are tasked to be the repository of knowledge on the world's small arms, and they are therefore trained on virtually every weapon likely to be found on operations anywhere in the world.

Their own personal weapon, how-ever, is the famed M16A1 rifle (the "Armalite") which has survived its period of controversy to become a very reliable and effective weapon.

Production of the M16A1 ended in 1975, but the US Army's stock is, in general, much older; the Army has twice put-off procuring new rifles, but is now almost certain to opt for the improved M16A2 and the Special Forces will be one of the earliest recipients. The M16A2 does away with the full automatic feature which enabled riflemen to blaze away using up vast amounts of ammunition, in favour of a 3-round burst capability.

A new barrel will make better use of the new standardised NATO 5.56mm round (which is slightly longer and heavier than the previous US 5.56mm round) and new sights will utilise this new capability better,

giving an effective range out to 875 yards (800m). Other, more esoteric small arms are on the drawing boards, but will not see service until after the year 2000.

Uniform

The basic hallmark of the Special Forces is the green beret, which was given to them by President Kennedy, and which has given rise to their nickname "the Green Berets". The cap-badge of the World War II 1st Special Service Force was the crossed arrows, which had previously belonged to the Indian Scouts, which had by then been disbanded. Today's Special Forces cap-badge combines these crossed arrows with a dagger which has a more than passing similarity to that of the British Special Air Service. The motto in the scroll surrounding the dagger is "De Oppresso Liber" ("Freedom from Oppression") which reflects their mission. This badge is normally set on a shield whose colours vary with the groups. A shoulder patch depicting the arrows is also worn on parade dress.

As with other special forces the basic uniforms are those of the US Army, although particular items may be added to fit in with a role. The Special Forces are, however, fairly high-visibility troops and tend not to act or dress covertly, leaving that to other, and more recently formed units.

Below: Green Berets "A Team" speeding towards their objective on board a River Patrol Boat (PBR). These water-jet craft have a speed of 24 knots and were widely used in the Vietnam War; some 500 were built.

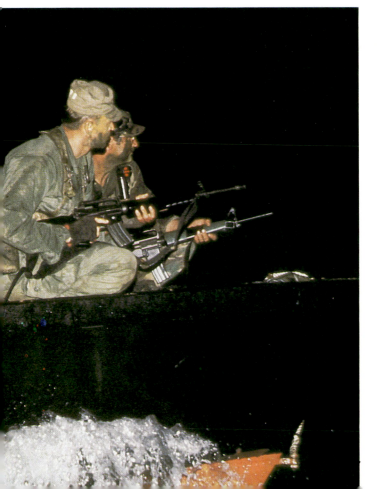

Marine Corps

The United States Marine Corps (USMC) is the world's largest elite force. With a strength of some 194,000 men and women in three divisions and three air wings with 416 combat aircraft it is even bigger then the total armed forces of most countries. Since it was raised by order of Congress on November 10, 1775, the USMC has taken part in every major war fought by the USA, as well as in numerous "police" actions and armed interventions all over the world. Its record is impressive and battles such as Belleau Wood, Guadalcanal, Iwo Jima, Chosin Reservoir, and Khe Sanh have earned it a special place in military history.

These fine traditions have merged to produce an amphibious assault force whose maintenance is the *raison d'etre* for today's corps. Further, the evolution of Marine aviation units has provided the Corps with its own air force (something which is a source of disagreement with the other services). This overall capability enables the USMC to claim to be a unique, combined-arms, ground-air force with a special competence in amphibious warfare.

The missions assigned to the USMC fall into three broad categories. The principal mission is to maintain an amphibious capability for use in conjunction with fleet operations, including the seizure and defence of advanced naval bases and the conduct of land operations essential to the successful execution of a maritime campaign. In addition, the Corps is required to provide security detachments for naval bases and the Navy's principal warships. Finally, the Corps carries out any additional duties placed upon it by the President.

A major feature of the USMC's position in the US defence establishment is unique in that it is the only service to have its basic corps structure defined by statutory law. The amended National Security Act of 1947 tasks the Marine Corps with maintaining a regular Fleet Marine Force of no less than three divisions and three aircraft wings, with the additional support units necessary. The USMC's very powerful lobby in Congress will ensure that it stays that way, too.

Organisation

Current active-duty strength of the USMC is some 194,000 (including 4,000 women), with some 38,000 reserves. These are organized into four divisions and four aircraft wings (three regular and one reserve of each), but both organisations are larger than their counterparts in the other services. This is particularly apparent in the division which, with a strength of 18,000 is some 20 per cent larger than a US Army division.

The basic structure of the Marine division is essentially the traditional "triangular" model, with three infantry regiments, each of three battalions. The new infantry battalion, however, is smaller than before, with a headquarters company, weapons company, and three rifle companies, each of the latter being 20 per cent smaller than

Current USMC Deployment	
3rd Marine Division (reinforced) 1st Marine Air Wing	Okinawa, but with one brigade in Hawaii.
1st Marine Division (reinforced) 3rd Marine Air Wing	Camp Pendleton, Ca. Cherry Point, NC.
2nd Marine Division 2nd Marine Air Wing	Camp Lejeune, NC. Cherry Point, NC.
4th Marine Division (reserve) 4th Marine Air Wing (reserve)	New Orleans, La.

their predecessors. Manpower and financial constraints prevented a fourth rifle company from being formed. Each Marine division has an artillery regiment, a tank battalion, an armoured, amphibian battalion, a light armoured assault battalion, (equipped with the new LAV), and other supporting units.

The standard Marine aircraft wing (MAW) has 18 to 21 squadrons with a total of 286 to 315 ▶

Above: US Marine in standard combat uniform. Note the "flak" vest and canvas "jungleboots". There are some 194,000 men and women in the USMC, making it one of the largest elite forces, and bigger than the total armed forces of many nations. Training is tough and discipline severe. The USMC also has a very strong lobby in Congress and a good image with the US public.

▶ aircraft, ranging from fighter/ attack (F-4, F-18), through medium attack (A-4, A-6, AV-8) and a tanker/transport squadron (KC-130), to helicopter squadrons (AH-1, CH-53, CH-46, UH-1) plus supporting squadrons of EW, observation and reconnaissance aircraft.

Weapons and equipment

The single dominant characteristic of Marine tactical doctrine is the emphasis on the principle of offensive action, which applies to all aspects of the Corps' activities. This ethos has a major effect on the way the USMC is equipped. Improved M16 rifles are being issued as the basic infantry weapon, while each squad, 11 strong, will soon have the new 5.56mm Squad Automatic Weapon (SAW) (M249) in each fire team. The battalion weapons company will also acquire a new heavy machine-gun platoon with eight firing teams, each of which will man a vehicle equipped with a 0.5in HMG and the new 40mm "machine-gun" (actually, a grenade launcher in all but name). An improved version of the 81mm

mortar is also about to be issued.

Changes are also underway in the artillery, aviation and armour capabilities of the corps. Three target acquisition batteries are being fielded over the next two years and the current 105mm and 155mm towed howitzers will be replaced by the new M198 155mm. There will also be an increase in the number of 155mm SP weapons, with five additional batteries being acquired over the next four years.

Marine aviation is being modernised. The controversial F-18 is now in service, while the AV-8B version ▶

Above right: M60A1 MBTs have been the mainstay of the USMC armoured force for many years and will remain till the 1990s.

Right: USMC gunner using an M2 Browning 0.50in (12.7mm) heavy machine-gun mounted on a tank-landing craft.

Below: USMC reconnaissance group hurry ashore with their inflatable boat. Such groups would usually land under cover of darkness.

▶ of the Harrier will reach squadrons in 1985. Two squadrons of CH-53Es, with a lift capacity of 16 tons, became operational in 1983. Unlike the Army, the USMC intends to keep its M60A1 MBTs in service until at least the end of the decade, but has ordered the Light Armored Vehicle (LAV) for use in the Light Armoured Assault Battalions (LAAB); there will be 145 LAVs in each LAAB with a total of 744 being purchased by the Corps.

Selection and training

All members of the US Armed Forces are now volunteers, and those for the USMC enlist direct into the Corps. Recruits go straight to one of the two training depots, at San Diego, Ca, and Parris Island, SC, where they undergo the famous 11-week "boot camp". This is an experience which all who undergo thoroughly appreciate once they have finished it, but that does not imply that anything would make them do it again!

Surprisingly, despite its size, the USMC does not have its own officer academy, although some are accepted from the Navy academy at Annapolis. The main source of officers is through the Naval ROTC, Officers Candidate School (OCS) or the Platoon Leaders Class. All officer candidates (including those from Annapolis) must undergo a rigorous selection and training course at Quantico, before being accepted for a commission.

The Mayaguez Incident May 12 1975

On May 12, 1975 a US ship, the SS *Mayaguez*, was seized by Cambodian gunboats in the Gulf of Thailand, 6½ miles off the island of Poulo Wai. The radio operator managed to transmit a message for help. President Gerald Ford quickly authorised firm action and on May 14 a 230-strong USMC group was flown from Okinawa to the USAF base at U-Tapao in south-east Thailand, which was some 223 miles (359km) from Koh Tang Island. The marines' transport to the operational area was to be provided by 14 USAF helicopters: seven HH-53 (code Jolly Greens, JG) and seven CH-53 (code Knife, K), although not all were available at the start of the operation. Both types were armed and protected with armour plate, but only the Jolly Green version could be refuelled in flight.

The nearest US Navy ship was the frigate USS *Harold E Holt*, which was fortuitously in the area, with the frigate USS *Henry B Wilson* and the fleet carrier USS *Coral Sea* steaming at flank speed from the north east, heading for the scene of the action.

The US forces knew that the *Mayaguez* was anchored 1½ miles (2.4km) north of Koh Tang island, but the whereabouts of the crew was uncertain. The plan was, therefore, somewhat open-ended:

Three helicopters would take some marines to the USS *Holt* to form a boarding party to retake the *Mayaguez*.

Eight helicopters would land a first-wave of marines at dawn on the northern beaches of Koh Tang to establish a base.

The second wave would then be flown to Koh Tang.

A third wave would be in reserve to exploit the tactical situation as it developed.

The battle

About 0645 (H-hour) two CH-53s —Knife 21 (K21) and K22—flew into West Beach, but as marines streamed over the lowered landing-ramp of K21 devastating fire was brought to bear at short range from enemy rifles, rockets and mortars. Surprise was total and one of K21's engines was damaged. Having offloaded its passengers, K21 flew off but had to be ditched a mile offshore. On the arrival of K32 and Jolly Green 41 (JG41), K22 headed back into the beach to land its marines; it was under fire the whole way in and suffered many hits, one of which caused a major fuel leak. Unable to land, K22 struggled to the mainland where it

Marine Air Wing

Aircraft Type	Function	Squadrons	Number of Aircraft
F-4, F-18	Fighter/Attack	4	48
A-4, AV-8A/B/C	Light Attack	2-3	38-57
A-6	Medium Attack	1-2	10-20
KC-130	Tanker/Transport	1	12
EA-6B	Electronic Warfare	1	4
RF-4	Reconnaissance	1	7
TAC-A	Tactical Air Control-Airborne	1	10
OV-10	Observation	1	12
AH-1	Attack helicopter	1	24
CH-53, CH-46	Transport/Utility	9	120
UH-1	Light Transport	6-7	131
Totals		28-31	416-445

A single Marine Air Wing has more tactical airpower than most national air forces, and the USMC has three active and another reserve MAWs!

made an emergency landing on the beach.

K32, fully loaded with passengers, dumped fuel before rescuing 3 of the 4 crew of the ditched K21 and then, accompanied by JG41, it flew to West Beach. Despite receiving 75 hits, including at least one from a rocket, K32 managed to land and offload its passengers, and then, with a

Below: May 15, 1975. A Marine and USAF pararescueman run to a USAF HH-53 helicopter during the Koh Tang operation. The refuelling capability was vital.

seriously wounded crewman, a wounded marine and the survivors of K21, returned to U-Tapao. JG41 was prevented from landing by the intense fire and eventually had to leave for an air-to-air refuelling from an HC-130P.

Events on East Beach followed a similar pattern, with K23 and K31 coming under heavy fire as they were about to touch down. K23 was hit in the rotor system and engines, and the pilot slammed it into the beach, ordering all 20 marines aboard to abandon the aircraft. K31 was also seriously damaged and the captain ditched ▶

▶ in the shallows; of the 26 on board 18 survived and escaped, but of these four were killed and one other died later. The survivors from K31 swam out to sea where all were subsequently rescued.

At sea the USS *Holt* had found the *Mayaguez*, but discovered that she was deserted. Thus, by H+1 hour the ship had been retaken (but without her crew), there were 25 men on East Beach (survivors from K23), 29 on West Beach, 13 were swimming out to sea, and of the 5 helicopters so far involved 3 had been destroyed, one ditched on the mainland and the fifth badly damaged.

Next to approach West Beach were JG42 and JG43 on their first run in, and JG41 returning from refuelling. JG41 was driven off with more hits, and then JG42 and JG43 were also forced back. JG43 flew down the coast and landed its 29 marines (including the CO) on a tiny LZ 875 yards (800m) to the south, although this proved of dubious value as they took many hours to fight their way back to join the main body. JG42, meanwhile, managed to land its marines on West Beach, but suffered heavy damage and had to return to U-Tapao escorted by JG43. JG41 then tried yet again to land its marines, but eventually had to go for yet another refuelling.

At about 0800 hours three more helicopters became available, but JG13 was immediately damaged trying to extract the 25 survivors of K23 from East Beach, and had to go back to U-Tapao. On West Beach JG41 had direct support from a C-130 Spectre gunship, including fire from a 105mm cannon. With this assistance the pilot brought JG41 in to land but came under mortar fire (including one bomb which passed through the rotor disc) and he flew off to refuel again with five passengers still aboard. He had been airborne for eight hours and was ordered back to base where his aircraft was grounded due to the extensive damage.

It was at this point that a local fishing boat returned the missing crew of the *Mayaguez* to the frigate

USS *Wilson*, having brought them from another island near the mainland. The Americans' aim then changed at once to retrieving the marines from Koh Tang, but this was easier said than done. The five remaining helicopters now approached Koh Tang with reinforcements. K52 tried to land but was hit repeatedly and her fuel tanks holed; since Knifes lacked an air-to-air refuelling capability the pilot had to return to the mainland.

On West Beach K51 and JG43, despite heavy fire, delivered their passengers, and K51 was even able to extract five badly wounded marines. JG43, still undamaged, met up with a circling HC-130P to take on yet more fuel. The second pair of helicopters (JG11, JG12) also succeeded in putting their marines ashore; JG12 took casualties aboard and departed for the mainland, while JG11 flew to the tanker, topped-up and returned at once to Koh Tang.

Meanwhile, the CO and his 29 men reached the West Beach main position, having fought hard all the way up, and with many captured weapons to prove it. Thus, at noon there were 222 men ashore, 197 on the West Beach, but with 25 still marooned on the East Beach. The larger force had managed to penetrate as far as a clearing half-way across the "Neck", but the Cambodians prevented any further progress. Another helicopter rescue was tried at about 1430 hours, following heavy bombardment and a CS gas attack (which failed due to contrary winds). JG43 was first in, but came under heavy fire and with heavy damage and several casualties was forced to limp off to the USS *Coral Sea*, by now some 70 miles (113km) away. JG11 then flew in, supported by fire from JG12, K51 and the USS *Wilson*'s long-barrel gun armed with two MGs. All 25 USMC and USAF men (helicopter crew) on the beach were taken off and flown to the *Coral Sea* and the focus of attention shifted to West Beach.

With darkness falling K51 went in under fire and rescued a full load of

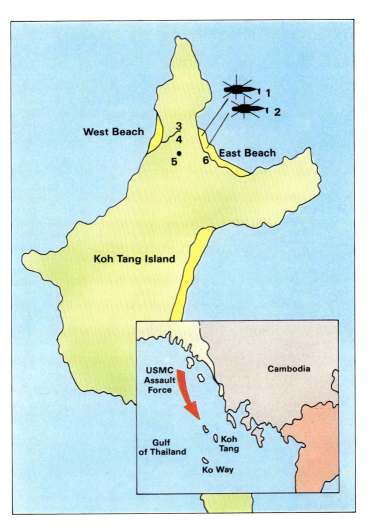

Above: The assault force was flown from Thailand. Two helicopters were shot down (1,2) and their crews pinned down (6).

Other landings on West Beach reached the clearings (3,4). AC-130 dropped a 15,000lb bomb (5) with no effect.

marines. JG43 then took on board 54 men, and both flew off to the *Coral Sea*. JG44 then went in, loaded up and took off, leaving 73 marines in a 50-yard (46m) perimeter on the beach, and under intense fire. JG44's pilot decided that the situation was so acute that he could save the 20 minute trip to the *Coral Sea* by landing his passengers on the USS *Holt*. With a crewman hanging out the door giving directions he got one main-

wheel on the corner of the flight-deck with only two feet (0.6m) of clearance for the rotor disc. He then returned to the beach, took off another load of marines but, due to engine power loss was forced to fly to the *Coral Sea*.

K51 returned quickly for the 29 marines remaining ashore. With 27 marines aboard a crewman had to run up the beach to grab the last two who were still giving covering fire at the jungle's edge.

SEALs and UDTs

The United States Navy Amphibious Forces include two types of special forces: Underwater Demolition Teams (UDT) and Sea-Air-Land (SEAL) teams. UDTs are the older organisation, having been raised in World War II. They perform traditional beach reconnaissance missions and are trained to destroy specific targets in the coastal area such as roads and bridges. They also carry out, as their name suggests, underwater demolitions, and their duties have also embraced the recovery of astronauts and space craft in the Mercury, Gemini and Apollo programmes.

All potential members of SEAL teams come from the ranks of the UDTs, and they receive extra training to prepare them for their new tasks. Their training differs primarily in that they are expected to operate with little support and in restricted waters, or on land in a combat environment where they may become involved in encounters with enemy forces.

To fulfil their mission SEALs may be carried to near the shoreline by a submarine, and leave it either on the surface or while submerged. They are also trained paratroops and could reach their operational area from land or carrier-based aircraft. Finally, of course, they could arrive by surface vessel.

Right: Member of a US Navy Underwater Demolition Team (UDT). UDTs date from World War II and are trained for beach recce and coastal operations.

Below: SEAL team on a beach reconnaissance in 1983. Nearest man is carrying the Stoner Mark 23 Commando MG, a weapon unique to the SEALs; a 5.56mm weapon, it is also known as M63.

▶ Organisation

US Navy regular special forces (there are more in the reserve) are controlled by Naval Special Warfare Groups (NAVSPECWARGRU). NAVSPECWARGRU 1 is based at the Naval Amphibious Base at Coronado, San Diego, California. Under its command are SEAL Team One, UDTs 11 and 12, Special Boat Squadron One (composed of Special Boat Units 11, 12 and 13) and Swimmer Delivery Vehicle (SDV) Team One. It also has administrative responsibility for Naval Special Warfare Unit One, located at Subic Bay in the Philippines. NAVSPECWARGRU 2 is at Little Creek, Norfolk, Virginia, with a similar composition, including SEAL Team Two and UDTs 21 and 22.

SEAL Teams each comprise 27 officers and 156 enlisted men, and UDTs 15 officers and 111 enlisted men. The SEAL Team is divided into five platoons, each of which is capable of self-contained operations.

Selection and training

Volunteers for UDTs must undergo a gruelling 24-week course. Training starts with four weeks of toughening runs, calisthenics and other physical preparation. Next comes several weeks of classroom work, exercises, open-sea swims, demolition work and recon- ▶

Above: SEAL team with an amazing variety of weapons, including Stoner Mark 23 Commando MGs and M16A1 rifles, both 5.56mm calibre.

Right: Members of UDT-21 on a swimmer delivery vehicle (SDV). UDT men must qualify in underwater swimming and combat, land operations and parachuting.

Below: Deep-Sea Rescue Vehicle-1 (DSRV-1) on a lowloader. This 32 ton vessel is designed for rescue, but could well also have a combat capability with UDTs.

naissance training. There is a one-week segment for escape-and-evasion, survival and land navigation training, followed by three weeks of airborne training and then underwater swimmer school.

SEALs take this training a stage further, and must also qualify in foreign languages, high altitude-low opening (HALO) parachute techniques. They also study the vagaries of unconventional warfare.

For their special skills and the hazardous nature of their duties UDT and SEAL personnel are paid extra. Officers receive $110 per month parachuting pay and a further $110 for demolition work. Enlisted men receive $55 for each of these tasks.

Weapons and equipment

The SEALs have in the past taken their own line on weaponry. In Vietnam they carried the Stoner M63A1 5.56mm machine-gun, an idiosyncratic weapon which needed extremely careful maintenance to work at its best; but at its best it was very good indeed.

Modern SEAL weapons include the US Navy Model 22 Type 0 9mm silenced pistol, developed by Smith and Wesson specially for the SEALs. Constructed throughout of stainless steel to prevent rust in the salt-water environment, the pistol is nicknamed the "Hush-Puppy", from its designed role of killing guard dogs.

Uniforms

There is no special uniform for UDT and SEAL personnel: they wear standard naval uniform with their own insignia, comparable to that of the naval air arm and submariners. On operations UDTs wear SCUBA gear appropriate to the operational environment. SEALs wear combat uniform, but tend to wear an olive-green scarf as headgear, rather than a hat, although the soft floppy "jungle-hat" is also seen. There is also a camouflaged beret.

Right: Static line parachute training for men of Underwater Demolition Team Twelve (UDT-12) at Subic Bay, Philippines.

Below: SEAL member up to his waist in mud, but still keeping his Stoner 5.56mm weapon clear. Only 35lb (16kg) with 800 rounds, it is a popular weapon.

Vietnamese Death Volunteers

The Vietnamese People's Liberation Army (VPLA) has been at war without a break since it was founded on December 22, 1944, by a then unknown history professor, Vo Nguyen Giap. This army has fought against the French, the United States and China, and has made its political masters the rulers of all Indo-China, as well as Laos and Kampuchea. In its campaign the VPLA may have lost battles, but it has never lost a war. Whatever else its opponents may have said against them, nobody has ever accused the soldiers of the VPLA of a lack of courage. But, outstanding among this company are the "Death Volunteers" who put themselves forward to carry out the most foolhardy actions, with the almost certain prospect of death, in order to demonstrate their loyalty and devotion to the Party.

The idea seems to have started about 1951 at a time when the VPLA was reorganising itself for major unit warfare against the French. Some battalions appreciated that it would be of value to have small groups of volunteers to carry out the most dangerous missions, and to lead the main attacks. The groups were formed and usually given the best equipment, such as the latest captured US sub-machine guns. In other armies a euphemistic title such as "commando" might have been used, but the VPLA, in its usual direct way, chose their very precisely descriptive designation.

Dien Bien Phu

The Death Volunteers made their presence felt in many battles against the French, but it was at the Battle of Dien Bien Phu (March 14-May 8, 1954) that they really made their mark. Platoons of these men blew gaps in the barbed-wire defences with plastic charges, and died in large numbers under the withering French fire.

Lest it be thought that these were merely ordinary line infantrymen of the VPLA, an extraordinary and well-documented example occurred on the evening of Saturday May 1, at the French position known as Eliane. Sergeant Kubiak of the Foreign Legion was on watch when he observed a ghostly figure, all in white, walking towards him through "no-man's land". A legionnaire brought the figure into the French position; he turned out to be a VPLA soldier swathed in a French white silk parachute, and he offered no resistance. Fortunately, Sergeant Kubiak recognised him for what he was and knocked him to the ground—the visitor was a Death Volunteer and under the parachute he had strapped to him some 50lb (23kg) of explosives which he was planning to detonate once he had got into the bunker. He was, in effect, a human bomb.

In the Second Indochina war such Death Volunteers appeared again, leading "forlorn hopes" or acting as rear-guards to protect withdrawing VPLA units. Numerous examples occurred of the latter, and to ensure that they did not falter in their self-imposed duty they often had themselves chained or roped to a tree in such a position that the enemy had to deal with them before going on. Such men are in the same tradition as the Japanese *kamikaze* pilots and the anonymous Arabs who drove lorries loaded with explosive into the US Marine and French positions in Beirut in 1983.

The concept of such coldly calculated and deliberate death is one which appears in only a few nations. Many elite forces appreciate that they will be at the forefront in the battle, but trust in superb training, self-discipline and initiative to get them through. Death is accepted as a risk, but is not greeted in quite this way such behaviour helps make the VPLA one of the most feared armies in all of Asia.

Right: This "death volunteer" of the Vietnamese People's Liberation Army has chained himself to a tree and will die resisting the enemy's advance.

Jungle hat

Locally produced
webbing equipment

Black
pyjamas

US-designed
0.45in M3
sub-machine
gun

Ammunition
pouch

Chains
attached to tree

sandals

153

GSG 9

When terrorist groups began operating extensively in Europe in the late 1960s the West Germans were very reluctant to be seen to form a dedicated anti-terrorist squad for fear of reviving memories of the Nazi regime. Such considerations were taken even further at the 1972 Munich Olympics where security was kept deliberately low-key in an attempt to promote a "pacific" image of the new Germany. Sadly, the West Germans were taught a dreadful lesson by the Black September terrorists who killed two members of the Israeli Olympic team and took nine others hostage. The West Germans staggered from crisis to crisis in their attempts to solve the problem, but it ended in tragedy when the nine hostages and the terrorists died together in a spectacular "shoot-out" at the Furstenfeldbruck military airfield.

Determined to avoid a further national humiliation, the West Germans created a totally new anti-terrorist group, but as part of the *Bundesgrenzschutz* (the Federal Border Police), and designated it *Grenzschutzgruppe 9* (GSG 9). This unit proved itself at Mogadishu in Somalia when a team of 27 men assaulted a hijacked Lufthansa airliner and released the 100-odd hostages. Since then there have been no overt GSG 9 operations, although there have been rumours of clandestine successes.

Organisation

Unlike virtually all other elite anti-terrorist units, GSG 9 is firmly a police unit, coming under the direction of the Federal Ministry of the Interior. It comprises a small HQ, four assault troops and a number of specialist sections, Current CO is Uwe Dee. The unit was 180 strong at the time of Mogadishu and as a result of that operation it was decided to increase it to 300, but recruiting difficulties keep strength at about 160 to 200. Nothing has been released of its internal organisation.

Selection and training

All members of GSG 9 must be volunteers from the ranks of the *Bundesgrenzschutz,* and thus any soldier in the *Bundeswehr* who wishes to join the unit must leave the Army and join the Border Police first. The training course is 22 weeks long and is dedicated to anti-terrorism. The first 13 weeks are devoted to police duties, legal matters, weapons skills and karate; ▶

Right: Counter-terrorist commando of West Germany's GSG 9, the elite unit of the Federal Border Police Force.

Below: The Border Police have their own aircraft to work with GSG 9. This Bell UH-1D is climbing away after dropping four men on an exercise.

German Army
pattern parachute helmet

Protective vest

Note absence
of badges/
symbols

9mm MPA5
Heckler and Koch
sub-machine gun

9mm P95
Heckler and Koch
pistol

155

Weapons and equipment

The basic weapon is the standard police sub-machine gun — the Heckler and Koch MP 9mm—but when used by GSG 9 it is fitted with a silencer. All men carry pistols and are allowed to select their own model, a rare degree of choice in such units. Most unusual of the weapons is the Heckler and Koch PSP 9mm P7 pistol which features a unique cocking device operated by gripping the gunframe —release it and the gun is totally safe!

Uniforms

GSG 9 wears standard *Bundesgrenzschutz* uniform — a green battledress with green beret. On operations the standard West German paratrooper helmet is worn, together with a flak jacket where necessary. No special unit identification is worn, although the wearing of a parachute qualification badge by a policeman may be an indication of his role.

Above: GSG 9 men practising entry to a railway carriage. Dutch security forces have had to deal with several incidents involving trains, although there have been none so far in West Germany.

▶ training takes place in a variety of locations as befits a unit which does not necessarily know in advance where it will be committed. The second part of the course comprises a detailed examination of terrorist movements combined with a final development of individual skills. Failure rate on the course is about 80 per cent. There is a stronger emphasis on academic work than in most such counter-terrorist units.

Above right: GSG 9 men, their faces obscured for security reasons, practise entry to a building. They are armed with 9mm Heckler and Koch MP 5 submachine guns.

Right: A training session for GSG 9. A special problem for such specialised units is the maintenance of morale and enthusiasm during long periods of training and rare action.

Mogadishu Rescue October 1977

The Red Army Faction, a hitherto unknown terrorist group, kidnapped Hans-Martin Schleyer, a leading West German businessman, on September 5, 1977. The terrorists demanded the release of 11 convicted terrorist comrades being held in West German jails, who were to be taken to Frankfurt Airport, and from there permitted to fly to "a country of their choice". West German Government negotiators could find no country willing to admit the terrorists and the crisis dragged on for over a month.

Then, at 1200 hours on October 13, a French radar operator saw on his screen a Lufthansa airliner suddenly change course. The aircraft captain, Jürgen Schumann, announced over the radio that his airliner, a Boeing 737 Lufthansa Flight LH 181, en route from Palam in the Balearic Islands to Germany had been hijacked by terrorists over the French Mediterranean coast. On board the aircraft were five aircrew (two pilots, three stewardesses), 86 passengers and four terrorists, two of them women.

The leader called himself "Captain Mahmoud", subsequently identified as a notorious international terrorist, Zohair Youssef Akache. He ordered Schumann to fly to Fiucimino Airport in Rome, where the airliner was refuelled.

From Rome, the airliner set off eastwards and landed at Larnaca in Cyprus at 2038. Here, "Mahmoud" demanded that the aircraft be refuelled again, or he would blow it up, the first of many such threats to use explosives. After refuelling the airliner took off again and overflew various Middle East countries. Permission to land at Beirut was denied and the runways were blocked, so it was taken on to Bahrein in the Persian Gulf where the same thing happened. It was flown onto Dubai where, despite being refused permission to land, the crew were forced to do so for lack of fuel.

At one point at Dubai the airliner lost power and the temperature inside rose to over 120°F (49°C); many of the passengers, some of them quite elderly, became very ▶

▶ distressed. While here the crew managed surreptitiously to signal that there were four hijackers to the local authorities.

Then, on Sunday October 16, the airliner suddenly took off, only 40 minutes before the first deadline for blowing it up. It was refused permission to land in Oman and arrived over Aden airport with sufficient fuel for another ten minutes' flying; despite the warnings of air traffic control, Captain Schumann brought it down safely on the taxi track.

By now conditions inside the aircraft were very bad, and "Mahmoud" was acting in an increasingly unpredictable and unstable manner. Schumann was allowed to leave the airliner to check the undercarriage and disappeared for a few minutes. When he returned he was taken to the first-class cabin and made to kneel on the floor; "Mahmoud" then shot him in the head, killing him instantly.

The next morning the co-pilot, Jürgen Vietor, took off and flew the airliner to Mogadishu, the capital of Somalia. There the German Government spokesmen contacted the hijackers and said that they were prepared to release the 11 prisoners held in jail and fly them to Mogadishu; "Mahmoud" postponed his deadline to 0245 hours the next morning (October 18).

The rescue

The West German crisis committee had already been dealing with the Schleyer kidnapping when the Lufthansa jet was hijacked and they simply switched from one problem to the other. A 30-strong contingent from GSG 9 was in the air within hours of the hijacking and arrived in Cyprus just as the Boeing 737 was taking off. Following a brief discussion with the Cypriot police the GSG 9 aircraft took off again and returned, via Ankara, to Frankfurt. Meanwhilte, a second aircraft containing Hans-Jürgen Wischnewski, West German Minister of State, psychologist Wolfgang Salewski, and another 30-strong group from GSG 9 led by their commander Ulrich Wegener had left West Germany and gone to Dubai. From there they went to Mogadishu, where they were given permission to land.

Below: The triumphant return of GSG 9 men from their operation in Mogadishu, which did much to restore German pride after the Munich debacle.

Press Association

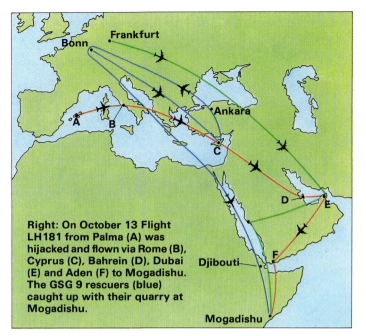

Right: On October 13 Flight LH181 from Palma (A) was hijacked and flown via Rome (B), Cyprus (C), Bahrein (D), Dubai (E) and Aden (F) to Mogadishu. The GSG 9 rescuers (blue) caught up with their quarry at Mogadishu.

In Mogadishu Wischnewski took over discussions with the hijackers, and as a 1600 hours deadline approached and it was clear that Mahmoud would in all probability carry out his threat to blow up the aircraft, the German Minister said that the 11 prisoners would be released. Mahmoud gave them until 0245 hours the following morning to produce the 11 at Mogadishu. At 2000 hours the first group from GSG 9 who had gone to Cyprus and then returned to Germany arrived in Mogadishu and the briefings began.

At 0205 hours, just 40 minutes before the expiry of the deadline, Somali troops lit a fire ahead of the aircraft. Two hijackers went to the cockpit to try to assess its significance, whereupon the tower contacted them by radio and started to discuss the conditions of the exchange which they said would commence in the near future, when the aircraft arrived from Germany with the released prisoners on board.

At 0207 precisely the emergency doors over the aircraft wings were blown open and members of the rescue party tossed in some "stun grenades". The men of GSG 9, with two British SAS men lent by the British government, had reached the plane and climbed onto the wings completely undetected; the hijackers (and the hostages) were taken completely by surprise.

The men of GSG 9 rushed into the aircraft shouting to the hostages to keep down on the floor, and opened fire on the hijackers. Mahmoud was fatally wounded in the first few seconds, but managed to throw two hand-grenades before he died; fortunately they were home-made and did no harm. One of the women terrorists died also and the second man was wounded inside the aircraft but died outside it a few minutes later. The second woman, Suhaila Sayeh, was wounded but did not die. Meanwhile the passengers were herded off the aircraft through the doors and emergency exits; none was seriously hurt. The operation ended at 0212 hours and was entirely successful. GSG 9 had proved itself and received a well-merited heroes' welcome when they returned to Germany. But three days later the body of Hans-Martin Schleyer was found in a car at Mulhouse.

OTHER SUPER-VALUE MILITARY GUIDES IN THIS SERIES......

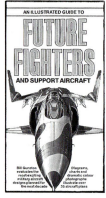

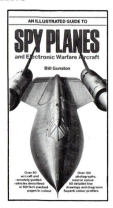

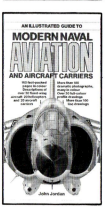

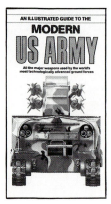

OTHER ILLUSTRATED MILITARY GUIDES NOW AVAILABLE.

Air War over Vietnam
Allied Fighters of World War II
Bombers of World War II
German, Italian and Japanese Fighters
   of World War II
Israeli Air Force
Military Helicopters
Modern Fighters and Attack Aircraft
Modern Soviet Air Force

Modern Soviet Navy
Modern Sub Hunters
Modern Submarines
Modern Tanks
Modern US Navy
Modern Warships
Pistols and Revolvers
Rifles and Sub-Machine Guns
World War II Tanks

* Each has 160 fact-filled pages
* Each is colourfully illustrated with hundreds of action photographs
   and technical drawings
* Each contains concisely presented data and accurate descriptions
   of major international weapons
* Each represents tremendous value

If you would like further information on any of our titles please write to:

Publicity Dept. (Military Div.), Salamander Books Ltd.,
27 Old Gloucester Street, London WC1N 3AF